THE
WOMAN IN ME

By
Minister Mrs. Bridget Benjamin

THE
WOMAN IN ME

Table of Contents

Introduction

The journey of understanding femininity and womanhood isn't a straightforward path. It twists and turns, reflecting the diverse experiences and perspectives of women across the globe. For anyone seeking to explore these complexities, this book serves as a beacon, illuminating the multifaceted nature of being a woman today. It is a tapestry woven from threads of stories, challenges, triumphs, and the enduring strength of women.

We live in a time where the question of what it means to be a woman is continually evolving. The roles and expectations surrounding womanhood are shifting under the weight of progressive thought, cultural shifts, and personal introspection. This book doesn't aim to provide definitive answers; rather, it seeks to empower you to find your own truth in the ever-changing landscape of gender and identity. Every woman's experience is unique, and yet there's an underlying connection that binds these varied stories together—a shared resilience and desire for authenticity.

There's power in storytelling. By sharing narratives, we give voice to the silent, strength to the weary, and hope to the lost. Our stories are the vessels through which wisdom is passed down and inspiration is ignited. This book draws upon the narratives of women from different walks of life, highlighting struggles, accomplishments, and dreams. By immersing ourselves in these stories, we bridge gaps, foster empathy, and build a community that transcends boundaries.

As you delve into these pages, you'll encounter a rich blend of cultural perspectives, showcasing how traditions and modernity intertwine to shape feminine ideals across the world. Society's expectations have long dictated what a woman's role should be, but today, more than ever, women are pushing back against these constraints, navigating gender norms, and overcoming stereotypes.

Personal growth and empowerment lie at the heart of this exploration. Women are embracing change, building inner strength, and nurturing relationships that are transformative. They are challenging beauty standards, celebrating diversity, and embarking on career paths that shatter ceilings and redefine success.

In understanding the intersectionality of womanhood, we cannot ignore the complexities of race, class, and gender. These factors play a crucial role in shaping one's experience and point of view. Acknowledging and amplifying the voices of the marginalized ensures that our vision for the future is inclusive and representative of all identities.

Ultimately, this book is about envisioning a future where femininity is fluid, diverse, and celebrated in all its forms. In this journey, may you draw inspiration and find empowerment, ready to contribute your voice and perspective to the ever-evolving narrative of what it means to be a woman in today's world.

Chapter 1:
Unraveling Identity

Identity, in its purest form, dances between the realms of self-discovery and societal expectation. While we find ourselves sifting through layers of who we are and who we're meant to be, the journey is anything but straightforward. It's a process, often messy and beautifully chaotic, that requires peeling back the veils of imposed identities to find the beating heart of authenticity within. In today's world, where gender roles are increasingly fluid and traditional norms are being renegotiated, the act of balancing these roles becomes an empowering declaration of individuality. As women embrace this uncharted terrain, they're crafting identities that are as diverse and unique as the myriad experiences that define womanhood. These stories of discovery and balance don't just enlighten; they embolden us to be unapologetically true to our essence, leaving a trail of courage and resilience for others to follow.

Discovering Authenticity

Authenticity, in its simplest form, is the alignment of our actions and words with our true selves. Yet, discovering it is often one of the most challenging and liberating journeys a woman can embark upon. It's a process that demands courage and introspection, a fearless dive into the depths of one's identity. As we unravel the threads of who we truly are, we encounter both stark revelations and gentle reminders of our unique blend of experiences, dreams, and values.

In a world that's constantly trying to define us through the lens of expectation, stepping into authenticity can feel revolutionary. It involves peeling back layers of societal norms, family expectations, and self-imposed limitations. It's about asking ourselves the powerful questions: Who am I beneath all these roles I perform? What do I believe when no one's watching? These questions are the compass that points us back to our true north.

For many, the journey to authenticity begins with a whisper of dissatisfaction—a sense that they're living an outer life that doesn't quite match their inner truth. This dissatisfaction isn't something to dismiss or run from. Rather, it's an invitation to explore, to listen closely to the softly-spoken desires and the stories we tell ourselves. Every word and thought is a thread that weaves the fabric of our authenticity, whether consciously or unconsciously.

At its core, discovering authenticity involves shedding the masks that have been worn to survive or fit in. Often, these masks are shaped by cultural narratives and ancestral voices that echo through generations. Young girls might be told to be "nice" and "agreeable," and those beliefs forge a path that can sometimes lead away from their true selves. It becomes crucial, then, to question these inherited stories and decide which ones to weave into our own evolving narrative.

In seeking authenticity, we also encounter vulnerability, standing in stark contrast to the curated personas social media perpetuates. It requires courage to present ourselves as we are—flaws, strengths, and all. But in doing so, we find freedom in self-acceptance and validation from within rather than from external sources. This shift in reliance can be profound, granting a sense of peace amid the chaos of external judgment.

Women across the globe are embracing this transformative journey, finding that authenticity is not just a personal endeavor but a communal one. As each woman steps into her true self, she offers others the permission to do the same, creating ripples of change that expand far beyond individual lives. These ripples break down barriers and connect us to a sisterhood that is rooted not in sameness, but in shared authenticity and mutual respect.

The challenge, however, lies in maintaining this authenticity in a world that often demands conformity. When the pressure mounts and doubts creep in, it's essential to remember that the quest for authenticity is not linear. It's a dance of two steps forward and one step back, chaotically beautiful and ever-evolving. Compassion for oneself during this process becomes a salve for the soul, allowing mistakes and missteps without shame.

For many women, mentorship and community support play pivotal roles in this journey. Having guiding lights—those who have walked the path before—can illuminate the trail. They offer insights and encouragement, showing that one's true self is not only valid but valuable. It's through shared stories and collective wisdom that we find strength and resilience to persevere.

Ultimately, discovering authenticity is an ongoing journey rather than a destination. What we uncover today about our true selves may shift and grow tomorrow. This fluidity is the beauty of authenticity; it allows for growth, change, and renewal. Embracing this ever-changing self requires flexibility and openness to new perspectives and experiences.

As we navigate this journey, let us hold space for both ourselves and others. In celebrating victories and acknowledging the struggles, we affirm the worthiness of each individual's path. Through this collective understanding, the limitations of the past are dissolved, and we find empowerment in writing our own narratives.

The story of discovering authenticity is as diverse and varied as the women who embark on it. Each experience brings a unique color to the tapestry of womanhood, revealing new facets of resilience and spirit. Together, as we share our truths and walk in alignment with our authentic selves, we carve out a more inclusive and understanding world, where every voice matters and every story holds power.

Balancing Roles

Women today navigate an intricate web of roles that often overlap, merge, and sometimes clash. Juggling careers, families, personal aspirations, and community responsibilities requires an innate flexibility—a dance of priorities that can leave one teetering on the edge of overwhelm. And yet, within this dazzling array of demands lies a unique opportunity to embody empowerment, even as challenges arise.

Consider the modern-day heroine, whose existence isn't defined by a single narrative. Her story isn't confined to being just a mother, just a leader, or just anything. Instead, she wears multiple hats, confidently switching her focus from the boardroom to the home, from caregiving duties to self-care rituals. This balancing act doesn't lessen her worth in any role—in fact, it magnifies her multifaceted nature.

Many women find themselves wrestling with expectations—both self-imposed and societal—in an ongoing quest to do it all. The pressure to excel in every domain can be relentless, tethering them to an ideal of perfection that is both alluring and exhausting. It's crucial to recognize that perfection is not the goal, but rather fulfillment in knowing that doing one's best, even if imperfect, is enough.

One profound illustration of finding balance is the adaptation to shifts in priorities that naturally occur over time. What serves us well at one life stage may not fit another, and that's okay. The transition from prioritizing career to focusing on family, or vice versa, doesn't signify loss. Instead, it's a reconfiguration—a reevaluation of where energy and passion are best directed to foster growth, create joy, and nurture self-worth.

Practical strategies can help manage these transitions with grace. Encouragingly, women are redefining success on their own terms. They're creating supportive networks, engaging in open dialogues about the struggles of balance, and sometimes, just allowing themselves the freedom to say no. The strength in honesty and vulnerability opens pathways to genuine support and camaraderie.

It's empowering to witness women empowering each other. By lifting one another, they challenge the dynamic that requires solitary achievement. There's beauty in collaboration, in shared stories of hardship and triumph, and in the collective courage that emerges when women support women. This reciprocity doesn't just ease individual burdens; it weaves a stronger societal fabric.

Another consideration in balancing roles is navigating the cultural expectations that shape perceptions of femininity and womanhood. In many cultures, the expectations collectivize women's identities into predetermined roles. Yet, as women consciously embrace and challenge these roles, they carve out spaces for individuality amidst societal constraints.

Empowerment also comes from setting boundaries, an often overlooked yet essential practice. Clear boundaries serve as the framework within which women can freely explore their multifaceted identities without fear of judgment or intrusion. This protective measure fosters a personal environment where growth and balance can flourish uninhibited.

Take, for example, the role of motherhood—it exists in the juxtaposition of immeasurable joy and ceaseless demand. Mothers, by necessity, develop remarkable agility in navigating this complex role. They sculpt environments conducive to raising compassionate, equitable future generations, often while pursuing their own passions. This nurturing instinct, blended with goal orientation, defines a modern balance: being present for oneself and for those in one's charge.

Yet, even with strategies in place, fatigue is inevitable. It's vital, culturally and personally, to normalize the acknowledgment of exhaustion without guilt. Sanctuaries must be created within daily life where women can recharge—whether through meditation, creative pursuits, or time spent with loved ones who inspire rather than drain.

As we reflect on the balancing roles women embody, there's a collective realization that no individual journey is identical. Some paths are linear, others circuitous, yet each holds a narrative that is wholly authentic to its traveler. The narrative weaves through ambition and rest, through power and gentility, each element equally valid and significant.

The future vision of balance involves an ongoing reevaluation of traditional gender roles, fueled by innovative and inclusive thinking. It acknowledges diversity, challenges stereotypes, and embraces change—welcoming deviations as opportunities for growth. Encouragingly, women today show an incredible capacity to redefine balance through their lived experiences and inherent wisdom.

Ultimately, balancing roles is about crafting a life that honors the whole self. It's about embracing the identity that thrives in the midst of contrasting demands. And it's about celebrating the journey of constant realignment, where each role becomes not a burden but a testament to strength and resilience—a vibrant tapestry of today's womanhood, both complex and complete.

Chapter 2:
The Power of Stories

Stories have a remarkable way of connecting us, revealing the threads that bind humanity through shared experiences and unique perspectives. They possess the ability to transform, to empower, and to ignite change within us. When women share their stories, the tapestry of womanhood becomes richer and more vibrant, filled with the truths and lessons of countless generations. These narratives are not just tales; they're life lines thrown to those navigating similar waters, encouraging them to keep rowing forward. As we listen to and learn from the stories of others, we find the courage to share our own, weaving new chapters into the ever-expanding book of womanhood. In these exchanges, we nurture a collective strength, a testament to the resilience and creativity inherent in every woman. Such power lies in the simple act of storytelling—an invitation to see the world through different eyes and, in doing so, to illuminate the multifaceted nature of being a woman today.

Sharing Women's Narratives

There's an undeniable power in sharing stories—an energy that transcends mere words to unite, inspire, and transform. When women come together to share their narratives, this power becomes even more palpable. It's as though every story told is a thread, woven into the fabric of collective understanding and empathy. Women's narratives, with their unique perspectives and diverse experiences, illuminate the landscapes of resilience, courage, and vulnerability.

Consider, for a moment, the quiet strength found in the whispered tales of grandmothers. These stories, passed from one generation to the next, carry the weight of survival and the joy of triumph. They are narratives that resist erasure and emerge defiantly, demanding to be heard and remembered. From tales of migration and adaptation to overcoming personal adversities, these narratives shape the younger women who listen to them, providing a compass in their life journeys.

Then there are the stories that come to life through the written word. In literature, women have carved out spaces to articulate their experiences, to protest injustices, and to celebrate victories. These written narratives often challenge societal norms, exposing the cracks where patriarchy tries to hide its flaws. They advocate for change, using the quiet force of storytelling to bulldoze barriers and incite reform. Our libraries and bookstores echo with the voices of women who refuse to be silenced.

In sharing these stories, we see how personal narratives can lead to broader conversations about universal truths. Women's narratives often contend with themes of identity, belonging, and resilience. They ask questions that ripple outward—What does it mean to be a woman in today's world? How do we reconcile the personal with the political? These questions, once stirred by individual stories, demand answers not just from women, but from all of society.

The influence of women's narratives extends beyond the individual and moves into the communal. Women who share their stories empower others to do the same, creating a ripple effect. Take the stories of those who have fought for rights and freedoms. Their narratives fuel movements, sparking activism and demanding that the world sit up and pay attention. Each account of struggle and resilience is a testament to the indomitable spirit of womanhood, an invincible force pushing against outdated norms.

There's also the transformative magic of hearing someone articulate feelings you've held silently. When a woman shares her story, it's often a mirror reflecting back common experiences. Struggles with identity, balancing familial and professional life, or navigating societal expectations—these are narratives so many recognize and resonate with. This shared recognition creates a network of solidarity, an invisible web that connects otherwise disparate lives.

We must also recognize the diversity in these narratives, as no two stories are identical. Women's experiences are colored by culture, race, socioeconomic status, and a multitude of other factors. By sharing varied narratives, we foster a more inclusive understanding of womanhood that embraces all its facets. It's in these differences that we find our richest lessons, and through these differences that empathy finds fertile ground.

Narratives of women from different cultural backgrounds highlight universal struggles while showcasing distinctive customs and traditions. These stories invite us to see life through different lenses. When a woman from another part of the world shares her journey, listeners are invited on a cultural excursion, opening their minds and hearts to a broader worldview. This exchange of stories doesn't just build knowledge; it cultivates respect and appreciation for global diversity.

Furthermore, sharing narratives is a radical act of self-assertion and self-preservation. In a world where women often find themselves marginalized, telling their stories becomes a way to reclaim their space and assert their right to exist boldly. It's a way to say, "I am here, and my story matters." Through storytelling, women affirm their presence and stake their claim in history—a history that's often been written without them.

The digital age has revolutionized how these narratives are shared. Social media platforms and blogs have given women new stages to tell their stories, bypassing traditional gatekeepers. This democratization of storytelling means that more voices, especially those previously unheard, are now part of the global discourse. Women are crafting their narratives in real-time, from #MeToo movements to personal vlogs, creating a rich tapestry of lived experiences for the world to see.

In listening to and sharing these stories, we find the empathy and understanding needed to build bridges in a divided world. Women's narratives, in all their forms, teach us about endurance and compassion, the power of speaking out, and the importance of listening. When we share and listen, we collectively write a new chapter for womankind—one that honors the past, celebrates the present, and inspires the future.

Ultimately, the power of sharing women's narratives lies in their ability to transform both the storyteller and the listener. These stories demand engagement, not just passive consumption. They urge us to action, inspiring us to create real change in our communities and the world. By giving voice to personal experiences, women don't just tell their stories; they open portals to understanding, healing, and transformation, paving the way for a more equitable and empathetic world.

Inspiring Through Experience

The power of storytelling is a remarkable force. Through stories, women have been able to communicate not just the bare facts of their circumstances, but the very essence of their experiences and the emotions interwoven with them. Many times it is through these narratives that we find the courage to understand both ourselves and one another. Every woman carries within her a tapestry of experiences that can be shared to inspire, heal, and empower those around her.

Consider the story of a woman who broke away from society's expectations to forge her own path. She may have faced doubts, been challenged by those around her, and stood alone at times. But in sharing her journey, she unleashes a message of resilience and determination. Her words, simple but profound, echo the inner strength she found amidst adversity, and that inspiration resonates deeply with those who hear her.

Life isn't just about the milestones we reach but the moments of vulnerability we embrace. Every woman knows a time when she was unsure, perhaps even scared. Sharing those moments is often one of the most potent ways to connect with others. Think about a young woman starting her career, burdened with uncertainty. Hearing from a mentor who navigated through similar experiences can provide insights beyond any training manual.

Empathy plays a crucial role in storytelling. It's about not just telling the facts, but conveying the emotions, creating a shared experience that transcends barriers. When women share their stories, they open a window into their world, inviting others to walk a mile in their shoes. This practice fosters understanding and reveals commonalities that exist beneath our diverse exteriors.

In every tale told, whether it's about balancing motherhood with career aspirations, overcoming personal losses, or championing causes larger than oneself, lies the potential to inspire change. Inspiration doesn't just prompt admiration; it stirs action, igniting a spark that motivates others to confront their challenges with renewed strength.

There is a unique power in intergenerational storytelling. A grandmother's account of her life's journey can inspire her granddaughter to pursue paths previously thought impossible. These narratives are more than just personal histories; they are legacies of wisdom, courage, and hope, handed down from one generation to the next.

Consider how stories intertwine with identity. They reveal the layers of womanhood that aren't always apparent on the surface. Through storytelling, we see how different aspects of identity are navigated—race, class, sexuality—and how they shape a woman's journey. Each story becomes a lens through which others can view their own experiences, helping to contextualize and better understand their personal narratives.

However, the impact of sharing experiences isn't solely beneficial to the audience. The storyteller herself undergoes a transformation. Articulating one's journey requires reflection, which can lead to personal growth. There's empowerment in speaking your truth, and there's liberation in knowing your story can influence and uplift others.

In a world where women's voices have often been marginalized, weaving together diverse narratives becomes an act of reclamation. It's saying, "This is who I am, and my story matters." And with every story shared, the collective voice of women's experiences becomes stronger, challenging outdated perceptions and broadening the understanding of what it means to be a woman today.

Breaking the silence around taboo topics can also be an incredibly potent use of storytelling. Whether it's discussing mental health, workplace discrimination, or bodily autonomy, the act of sharing provides solace to those who felt isolated in their struggles. These narratives not only inspire but also educate and advocate, coaxing necessary conversations into the open.

Ultimately, the power of storytelling lies in its capacity to unite. It reminds us that while each woman's experience is unique, the threads of happiness, heartbreak, triumph, and loss are universal. They are felt by all. Through the articulation of personal experiences, women create a tapestry of shared humanity—a rich and colorful narrative painting a fuller picture of womanhood for all to see and feel.

So let us encourage women to continue sharing their stories, no matter how big or small. Let's foster a culture where these narratives are not just heard but celebrated for their authenticity and ability to bring about change. The potential to inspire through experience is limitless, and with every story told, the world becomes a bit richer and more understanding of the broad spectrum of our collective experiences as women.

Chapter 3:
Cultural Perspectives on Womanhood

Entering the vibrant tapestry of cultural perspectives on womanhood, we uncover an intricate dance between tradition and modernity, where women across the globe inhabit roles both defined and defied by the cultures they are part of. The journey to grasp these diverse cultural ideals isn't just about learning; it's about feeling the threads of shared struggles and triumphs that bind us. In one corner of the world, womanhood might be cloaked in layers of ancestral customs, each thread holding deep-rooted significance, while elsewhere, it unfolds in the vibrant hues of modern aspirations, crafting new narratives of self-expression and autonomy. Amidst these diverse backdrops, we see women weaving personal identities with cultural expectations, balancing reverence for the past with the courage to step boldly into the future. This journey through culture illustrates one undeniable truth: womanhood is as varied and expansive as the cultures that celebrate it, a testament to the resilience and adaptability of women who gracefully navigate these complexities with strength and grace.

Traditions and Modernity

The dance between tradition and modernity is a complex choreography, and when it comes to womanhood, it becomes a unique blend of heritage and innovation. Caught between these two realms, many women find themselves negotiating a precarious balance. Tradition, with all its rich cultural tapestry, is an anchor, a link to the past. Modernity, on the other hand, pushes the boundaries, urging women towards new horizons. This section explores how women navigate this intersection, discovering their place within a world that is continuously redefining itself.

In some parts of the world, traditions still hold a dominant role, defining pathways for women that have been walked for centuries. These traditions often come with particular expectations and roles that prescribe what it means to be a woman. While there's a deep sense of pride and identity in adhering to these traditions, they can occasionally become constraints rather than sources of empowerment. The challenge lies in preserving the essence of these traditions while allowing room for growth and change.

Imagine a woman who grew up in a rural village, steeped in traditions that celebrate community and family bonds. Her upbringing was a tapestry of ancient rituals and beliefs, yet she hungers for the education she knows can transform her life. She envisions a future where these traditions can coexist with a career that takes her beyond the horizons her ancestors knew. This is the heart of the woman's journey, marrying heritage with ambition.

As the world becomes more interconnected, modernity challenges tradition, introducing ideals of independence and personal achievement that clash with communal values. This tension becomes particularly pronounced in societies where gender roles are deeply rooted. Here, women face the dual task of honoring their cultural legacies while asserting their agency in modern contexts.

Yet, it's not just about struggle. The fusion of these worlds can create something beautiful and empowering, offering women the opportunity to redefine aspects of tradition in a way that aligns with contemporary values. For instance, women are increasingly taking control of traditional practices that once confined them. Rituals that dictated certain roles are now being reimagined to celebrate women's autonomy and strengths.

Consider the re-envisioning of marriage ceremonies in several cultures where brides choose their paths with equal say or even opt for intimate ceremonies that emphasize partnership over formality. These shifts reflect a broader change, where tradition is not discarded but transformed into a vessel that carries modern aspirations.

The presence of technology also plays a significant role in this dynamic. With access to global information, women discover new perspectives and possibilities. Social media platforms become tools for connection, support, and advocacy, allowing women to share stories of breaking free from tradition or reforming it in meaningful ways.

At the heart of this paradox is a truth: traditions offer roots, but modernity offers wings. Women today are crafting identities that embrace both, forging paths that are uniquely their own. They are storytellers of a new narrative where they are empowered to choose which customs to keep, revise, or let go entirely.

However, this journey isn't without its conflicts and challenges. Sometimes, the grip of tradition is strong, particularly for those who face societal pressures to conform. Modernity, with its promise of progress and emancipation, may seem seductive, yet it's peppered with its own set of expectations and pressures. The key lies in striking a balance that's personal and authentic.

The power of redefining tradition lies within the individual woman deciding how she honors her past while shaping her future. Every woman has her own timeline and map, crafted with her experiences, dreams, and aspirations. As such, the intersection of tradition and modernity isn't a battleground but a landscape of possibility.

Women around the globe are exemplifying resilience as they navigate these complexities, choosing to embrace and redefine what it means to uphold tradition while stepping confidently into the modern world. They are crafting a narrative that is both inclusive of their heritage and reflective of their ambitions.

In this delicate dance, the exchange between tradition and modernity presents a vibrant opportunity for growth, reflection, and empowerment. The journey is ongoing—a testament to the strength and adaptability of women as they continue to navigate the rivers of change, finding strength in both roots and wings.

Feminine Ideals Across Cultures

In the rich tapestry of cultures around the world, the notion of femininity takes on a multitude of forms, each colored by history, tradition, and societal norm. It's fascinating to consider how these diverse perspectives paint a broader picture of womanhood. While femininity often centers around ideals shaped by cultural narratives, it's important to recognize the beauty in its variations. The concept transcends borders and yet ties women across continents, speaking to a shared experience influenced by individual context and community values. Every culture has its own unique way of defining and celebrating what it means to be a woman.

In Asia, for instance, the ideal feminine has often been associated with grace, humility, and resilience. These values are deeply rooted in historical contexts where women have traditionally played pivotal roles within their families and communities, often maintaining harmony and balance in their households. This expectation for women to embody a gentle strength is embodied through cultural icons and literature over centuries. However, this has not quelled the fire that burns within many to break boundaries; modern women are increasingly challenging these traditional roles, weaving their own narratives, and broadening what it means to embrace femininity.

Similarly, in Latin America, the embodiment of Marianismo—a counterpart to the machismo culture—has traditionally placed women in roles of self-sacrifice, nurturing, and spiritual fortitude. Yet, as society evolves, many are asserting themselves beyond these confines. The rising tide of feminism is fostering a new form of femininity, one that honors traditional values while challenging the patriarchal framework. Women here are increasingly seen as leaders and changemakers, actively participating in political arenas and community development while embracing the ethos of collective empowerment.

African cultures provide another intriguing lens through which femininity is viewed. Here, women have often been seen as the backbone of their communities, not only as caretakers but also as central to economic and social structures. The strength and power attributed to African womanhood are intertwined with motherhood and community service. Importantly, in many African societies, femininity is revered through oral traditions and stories passed down through generations, highlighting the pivotal roles women play. Yet, there remains an ongoing negotiation between maintaining cherished traditions and embracing modernity's promise of gender equality and independence.

European ideals, on the other hand, have experienced a shift from stringent Victorian norms to a more inclusive and liberated understanding of femininity. Western Europe, in particular, with its push towards gender equality, envisions femininity through lenses of independence and individuality. Although not without its struggles to eradicate old stereotypes, the emphasis is stronger than ever on women's rights and personal choice, celebrating the capacity and agency of women to determine their own paths.

Despite the varied expressions of femininity, there's a universal allure in the endeavor to break free from the connotations that no longer serve contemporary women. The process takes courage, as traditions, no matter how binding, lie at the heart of people's identities. However, as women globally push against the boundaries set around them and forge new pathways, they're rewriting what it means to embody femininity. This redefinition, steeped in passion and resilience, refuses a singular narrative, choosing instead to introduce a broader spectrum of possibilities.

Each of these perspectives highlights the intricate linkage between the personal and the collective narratives women weave, influenced by cultural ideologies and traditions that shape individual identities. The dynamic nature of femininity reflects an ongoing journey—a living dialogue between past, present, and future, promising an expansive vision where all voices are heard. It's a testament to the strength and adaptability inherent in womanhood, capable of thriving against the most demanding backdrops and embracing the potential for transformation.

So, let us be inspired by these stories of women who pursue authenticity within their cultural contexts and beyond them. Their journeys are not merely about challenging the status quo but also celebrating the rich complexities of what it means to be a woman in the world today. Ultimately, femininity across cultures stands as a powerful reminder of the common threads of resilience, strength, and compassion that connect women everywhere, creating a mosaic that is as diverse as it is beautiful, reflecting both unity and individuality.

Chapter 4:
Society's Expectations

In the intricate dance of societal expectations, women find themselves navigating a landscape that's been shaped by century-old norms and modern-day ideals. It's as if society hands out roles like scripts, expecting each woman to perform flawlessly. Yet, within these confines, there's an unyielding desire to break free and redefine what it means to be a woman today. With every stereotype dismantled and every norm questioned, women are not merely rebelling against a one-size-fits-all mold; they're carving out spaces where individuality is celebrated, not suppressed. The bravery to challenge these expectations transforms this journey into one of self-discovery and empowerment, where the courage to be authentic opens doors to a future where all forms of womanhood are embraced and honored.

Navigating Gender Norms

In society, gender norms act as the invisible traffic signs, subtly directing behavior and decisions at every crossroads of life. These norms are complex and deeply woven into the cultural fabric, shaping expectations about what it means to be a woman. For many, they present a winding journey—sometimes full of obstacles, yet brimming with opportunities for growth and redefinition. The challenge lies in navigating these norms while staying true to one's authentic self.

Women worldwide live under the shadow of prescribed gender roles, often facing conflicting expectations. There's an unspoken script that seems to dictate how femininity should be expressed. It's an intricate dance, balancing between fulfilling traditional expectations and pursuing personal aspirations. It demands not just skill but courage—to challenge the script and to sometimes write new lines.

The impact of gender norms is felt from a young age. Many girls grow up with subtle, sometimes overt, cues about what's acceptable and what's not. "Act like a lady," "Be polite," and "Dress appropriately" are phrases quietly whispered by older generations, their emphasis varying across cultures, yet their intent to mold behavior constant. The results can be confining, stifling individuality and deterring personal freedom.

However, the narrative is changing. More voices are advocating for a broader understanding of what it means to be a woman. In cities and villages, from boardrooms to classrooms, there's a gradual revolution. Women are taking control of their stories, refusing to be limited by antiquated norms. This revolution is both a collective movement and an intensely personal journey.

Breaking free from these norms is not just about defying societal expectations but also involves internal battles. It calls for unlearning and relearning—to trust one's instincts, to embrace imperfections, and to pursue passions without fear or apology. This path is neither straightforward nor easy. Yet, it is profoundly empowering, as each step forward crafts a narrative of resilience and strength.

Consider the story of Malala Yousafzai, a young woman who defied expectations in a society where female education was undervalued. Her journey transcended national boundaries, challenging the world to rethink gender norms and values. Malala's narrative is a testament to the power of individuals to create space for new norms, where education and empowerment are not gendered privileges but universal rights.

Another striking example comes from the corporate world, where women are continuously breaking norms to carve out spaces for themselves. Slowly but surely, the glass walls and ceilings are shattering. These women are redefining what leadership looks like, asserting that empathy and strength are not mutually exclusive, and that assertiveness does not compromise femininity.

In acknowledging these shifts, it's essential not to overlook the role of men in navigating gender norms. Change is not a solitary journey but a joint endeavor. When men actively participate in redefining gender expectations, they contribute to the broader tapestry of equity. Allies in this journey open doors to dialogues that challenge stereotypes and create new possibilities for everyone.

The work of navigating gender norms is ongoing, a journey without a final destination. With each generation, new interpretations and modifications will emerge. Today's actions lay the groundwork for tomorrow's narrative, a tale passed down not in whispered commands but in shared stories of empowerment.

Ultimately, the task for many women remains clear: to be unapologetically authentic in a world eager to impose labels and limitations; to engage in a lifelong dialogue between expectations and aspirations. Though the path may be fraught with challenges, the rewards of self-discovery and personal empowerment are immeasurable.

Overcoming Stereotypes

Society is an intricate tapestry of beliefs and expectations, often constricting individuals within the confines of stereotypes. Especially for women, these stereotypes can be pervasive, dictating how they should behave, appear, and even think. The journey to overcoming these stereotypes is not just one of resistance, but of rewriting narratives, creating spaces for authentic expression, and encouraging a deeper understanding of what it means to be a woman in the modern world.

A stereotype, at its core, is a singular story that gets told repeatedly until it drowns out all other possibilities. When we say women are nurturing, for instance, it doesn't mean they are incapable of being strategic or competitive. The problem arises when the world sees women only through the lens of a few tired stereotypes, limiting their potential before it even has a chance to emerge. To overcome these clichés, society needs to embrace complexity and diversity in womanhood.

Imagine the weight lifted when a woman realizes she doesn't have to fit into a predefined box. It's a moment of revelation, often accompanied by the quiet determination to forge her path. Overcoming stereotypes is about reclaiming agency—it's about saying, "I get to decide who I am." This self-authored identity isn't just liberating; it's empowering for both the woman herself and those around her.

Consider the pressure that young girls face when growing up. They're told "girls shouldn't be assertive" or "women aren't as good at math." These social scripts can be internalized and become barriers to pursuing interests and passions outside the traditional scope. The path to overcoming these stereotypes begins in education and mentorship. By celebrating female role models in diverse fields—from scientists to artists to leaders—young women are shown that their dreams are valid and their aspirations attainable.

Creating spaces where stereotypes can be challenged requires collective societal effort. Workplaces, educational institutions, media, and communities need to commit to dismantling outdated norms and actively promote inclusivity. It's not just about adding a few diverse faces to a group; it's about valuing the unique perspectives and contributions each person can bring. Through this lens, diversity becomes a wellspring of innovation and progress rather than a checkbox to be ticked.

On an individual level, combating stereotypes takes courage and resilience. It often involves speaking up, even when your voice quivers, and advocating for yourself and others. It means making choices that resonate with your authentic self, rather than succumbing to the chorus of societal expectations. It requires embracing vulnerability and sharing your unique story to inspire others to confront their challenges.

Yet, in this struggle, women are never alone. Across the globe, countless women have broken through glass ceilings, defied expectations, and redefined what it means to succeed. Their stories become beacons of hope and pathways for others to follow. In by supporting each other, women create networks of solidarity that transform individual achievements into a collective force for change.

Conversations play a pivotal role in overcoming stereotypes. When women engage in dialogues about their experiences, they expose the limitations of stereotypes and highlight the rich diversity of womanhood. These conversations should happen in living rooms, boardrooms, classrooms, and on global platforms. As these narratives spread, they shift cultural perceptions, gradually uprooting the stereotypes that once seemed immovable.

Equally critical is the role of men in overcoming stereotypes. When men become allies in this journey, they help dismantle the patriarchal structures that perpetuate these limiting narratives. By championing gender equality, men not only contribute to a more just society but also liberate themselves from the constraints of rigid masculinity.

Ultimately, overcoming stereotypes is about rewriting the story of womanhood. Instead of seeing women through the narrow lens of societal expectations, the focus shifts to celebrating their intricate identities. It's a journey toward breaking free from the chains of the past and stepping into a future where every woman can be wholly herself, with no need for apologies or justifications.

This journey is ongoing and requires unwavering commitment. It calls for a willingness to confront discomfort, challenge bias, and celebrate progress in all its forms. By doing so, society can create a world where the only limits women face are the ones they choose for themselves—where a woman can define her path and, in doing so, inspire others to do the same.

Let us envision this world together. A world where the strength and spirit of women are honored, where their voices are heard, and where stereotypes are left in the dust of history. In this world, every woman walks her path with confidence, knowing that she is seen, valued, and celebrated for who she truly is.

Chapter 5:
Personal Growth and
Empowerment

Venturing into the realm of personal growth and empowerment is akin to embarking on an ever-evolving journey where every step fortifies the spirit and expands the mind. Here, women embrace change, even when it's daunting, recognizing it's often the catalyst for profound transformation. As layers of self-doubt peel away, and the cacophony of societal expectations fades, what emerges is a clarity that enables them to build inner strength. This newfound power fuels resilience and fosters a sense of autonomy, allowing women to assert their voices and chart their own paths. This chapter isn't just about breaking free from old constraints but also about celebrating the newfound freedom to redefine personal narratives. The echoes of past limitations no longer dictate the scope of their aspirations; instead, they stand rooted in their authenticity, poised to inspire others as they embrace the boundless potential of what lies ahead.

Embracing Change

Change is an inevitable companion, constantly nudging us forward or pulling us back, but it's how we respond to it that defines our journey through life. For women navigating the intricate tapestry of modern-day womanhood, embracing change with open arms can become one of the most empowering decisions ever made. While change often comes with the weight of uncertainty, it simultaneously provides an unparalleled opportunity for growth and self-discovery.

One can't talk about embracing change without acknowledging the myriad of feelings it stirs. From excitement to fear, optimism to doubt, every emotion is valid and offers insights into our inner landscapes. These emotions, though sometimes overwhelming, are not meant to be deterrents. Instead, they're signposts pointing us towards areas that need our attention and care. Understanding and confronting these feelings can be liberating, serving as stepping stones to a more profound personal transformation.

Throughout history, change has been both a force of creativity and disruption. It has allowed women to forge paths previously deemed unimaginable, from securing the right to vote to breaking boundaries in fields traditionally dominated by men. These monumental shifts reflect the collective power of women who chose to embrace change, illustrating the profound impact that individual courage can have when it converges with broad social currents.

Embracing change does not imply reckless abandonment of all that is familiar or cherished. Rather, it involves a conscious acceptance of new possibilities and the courage to make decisions that align with our true selves. This alignment fosters authenticity, allowing us to navigate our roles and identities with greater freedom and less fear of judgment. When women embrace change, they redefine resilience, finding strength in vulnerability and beauty in imperfection.

In the pursuit of personal growth, embracing change acts as a catalyst that propels us beyond comfort zones. The challenges that accompany change fine-tune our resilience and enhance our ability to adapt. It is in these moments of adaptation that we discover capacities we never knew we had, rewriting the narrative of what it means to be a woman in today's ever-evolving world.

No two journeys through change are alike; each is as unique as the individual experiencing it. It's essential to recognize that the path is neither linear nor predictable. There will be setbacks and triumphs, both of which are integral to the process. The willingness to embrace change requires patience and self-compassion, acknowledging that every step, regardless of size, holds significance in the broader spectrum of personal growth.

Stories of women who have embraced change can be deeply inspiring. Take, for example, the woman who leaves an unfulfilling career to pursue her passion for art. Despite societal pressures to conform to a stable and conventional path, she listens to the whispers of her heart, choosing the exhilarating uncertainty of following her dreams. Her journey is not just about creating art; it is about redefining success on her terms, demonstrating that change can lead to deeper fulfilment and joy.

Another poignant illustration is the mother who redefines her identity after her children leave home. Initially confronted with a sense of loss, she utilizes this transitional phase to explore new interests and reconnect with her individuality. Through embracing this change, she not only enriches her own life but also models adaptability and self-awareness to her children, showing it's never too late to reinvent oneself.

The fear of change is a natural instinct, often rooted in the desire for security and certainty. Yet, by reframing our perspective on change—from something to be feared to something to be welcomed—we can begin to appreciate the gifts it brings. With this shift in mindset, women can harness the potential of change as a tool for empowerment, breaking free from the constraints of societal expectations and forging new paths tailored to their ambitions and desires.

While change can be daunting, one must remember that it is not navigated alone. Building a support network of like-minded individuals provides a safe space to share experiences, gain insights, and offer encouragement. This sense of community strengthens our resolve, reminding us that while the journey is personal, the experience is universal.

As women continue to embrace change, they contribute to a collective evolution, challenging antiquated stereotypes and crafting narratives that resonate with authenticity and empowerment. In this way, change is not just a personal journey but a communal movement toward greater equality and understanding, encouraging future generations to embrace it with hope rather than hesitation.

Ultimately, the act of embracing change transforms more than just our lives; it influences the world around us. Each step taken in confidence and courage paves the way for others to follow, creating ripples of change that expand beyond our immediate surroundings. By welcoming change, women not only grow individually but also contribute to a more dynamic and inclusive understanding of femininity worldwide, where the complexities of womanhood are celebrated rather than constrained.

Building Inner Strength

Inner strength is a vast reservoir, often hidden beneath the surface, waiting to be discovered and harnessed. It's that resilient thread woven into the fabric of womanhood, allowing women to navigate life's myriad challenges with grace and determination. Building this strength begins with the acknowledgment that it's an ongoing journey, one that demands patience and self-awareness.

There's a certain beauty in recognizing our vulnerabilities. They remind us that being strong doesn't mean the absence of fear or doubt but the courage to face them head-on. For many women, the realization that self-compassion is a vital component of inner strength can be revelatory. Embracing our imperfections grants us the freedom to grow beyond them, to mold our experiences into a wellspring of wisdom and power.

Women across times and cultures have shared a universal understanding of resilience. Whether it's whispered wisdom passed down through generations or lessons learned from life's crucible, these shared experiences create a rich tapestry of strength. We carry the lessons of our foremothers, who stood resolute against the tides of adversity, forging paths where there seemed to be none.

Inner strength is also about nurturing a deep connection with oneself. It's about carving out moments amidst our busy lives to listen to our inner voices. Many women find solace and strength in practices like meditation, journaling, or simply spending time in nature. These quiet reflections become the fertile ground where seeds of strength can take root and flourish.

In building inner strength, challenges often become our greatest teachers. Each setback or obstacle encountered reveals hidden layers of resilience we might not have known we possessed. The ability to stand firm in the face of adversity, to rise from each fall with renewed conviction, is a testament to the indomitable spirit of womanhood.

But inner strength doesn't thrive in isolation. It's nurtured through the bonds we form, the communities we build, and the support we offer and receive. Women's circles—both literal and metaphorical—become havens where stories of strength are shared, where triumphs and trials are met with understanding and encouragement.

At times, building inner strength requires us to redefine our understanding of success and failure. It's seeing beyond the binary of victory and defeat and embracing the journey itself. Each step forward, whether tentative or bold, is a testament to our resilience.

Education can be an empowering tool in this journey. A thirst for knowledge, for understanding the world and our place within it, fuels our inner fires. Whether it's mastering a new skill or exploring uncharted areas of interest, each new piece of wisdom adds to our reservoir of strength.

And yet, building inner strength is deeply personal and uniquely individual. It doesn't follow a prescribed path or conform to a specific blueprint. It requires us to be gentle with ourselves, to acknowledge that each of our journeys is different and equally valid.

The stories of countless women illustrate how pivotal moments of self-discovery serve as catalysts for building strength. For some, it's a turning point catalyzed by personal upheaval; for others, it's a gradual awakening nurtured in the everyday. These stories become beacons, guiding us through the labyrinth of life.

We've come to understand that inner strength is not merely about survival—it's about thriving. It's crafting a life that reflects our deepest values and aspirations. As women, we learn to harness our intuition, to trust in that silent wisdom that propels us forward, urging us to remain steadfast even when the path is uncertain.

In the end, building inner strength requires a delicate balance between vulnerability and resilience, between surrender and tenacity. It's the quiet yet resolute voice within that dares us to dream, to pursue our passions with vigor, to stand tall in our authenticity.

As we reflect on the process of building inner strength, we're reminded of its boundless potential. It's a lifelong pursuit, ever unfolding, and intimately interwoven with the broader journey of personal growth and empowerment. It serves as both a formidable shield and a potent source of power, guiding us through the intricacies of being a woman in today's world.

May we continue to foster this strength within ourselves, drawing inspiration from those who have gone before, and lighting the way for those who will follow. Together, we build a legacy of resilience, courage, and unwavering strength, a testament to the enduring spirit of femininity.

Chapter 6:
Relationships and Connection

In the intricate dance of relationships, women find a canvas where their strengths, vulnerabilities, and resilience all converge to paint a vivid portrait of connection. It's in these interactions that we discover the heart's ability to both shatter and heal, crafting a tapestry rich with empathy and understanding. Relationships can be a sanctuary, where camaraderie flourishes and bonds strengthen through empathy's gentle embrace, reminding us that our connections are not just our shared stories but the bridges leading to profound personal growth. In every whispered secret, every shared laughter, and even in moments of conflict, lies the opportunity to nurture bonds that are both grounding and liberating. By fostering empathy, we transform these connections into spaces where authenticity thrives and where the multifaceted essence of womanhood is celebrated in all its glory.

Nurturing Bonds

As we journey deeper into the tapestry of womanhood, the intricate web of relationships emerges as a central theme. Nurturing bonds form the bedrock of our existence, influencing our well-being and defining our sense of belonging. In a world that often emphasizes independence, we mustn't undervalue the power of connection—a crucial aspect of our shared humanity.

Relationships are not simply interactions; they are the essential fibers that knit our lives together. Whether with family, friends, or romantic partners, these connections provide emotional sustenance and resilience during life's challenges. The art of nurturing these bonds requires patience, empathy, and understanding. Each relationship is a unique fingerprint, shaped by the individuals involved, and yet, the principles that guide their nurturance are universal.

Bonds with family can be our first exposure to love and support. They shape our earliest perceptions of trust and safety. For many, these ties offer a foundation of unwavering support. Yet, even familial relationships demand attention and care. A daughter's relationship with her mother, for example, often oscillates between moments of friction and warmth, yet it remains pivotal. It is in these relationships that we first learn to balance our desires with those of others, developing a map for navigating life's interactions.

Friendships, on the other hand, are the chosen family members in our lives. Friends see us through the eyes of acceptance, valuing us outside the constraints of blood ties. These relationships are formed through shared experiences and mutual respect, weathering the tests of time. Forging deep friendships demands openness and vulnerability—a willingness to show our true selves and in return, accept others as they are.

Romantic relationships often carry the greatest expectations and, sometimes, the deepest disappointments. They are filled with passion and challenge, transcending mere companionship. The journey of love requires unrelenting communication, compassion, and mutual respect. Successful romantic bonds blossom through shared dreams, nurtured by a partnership that recognizes and champions the individuality within the union.

Nurturing these relationships requires understanding the cycles they undergo. As we move through different stages of life, so too do our needs and expectations from these bonds evolve. It is crucial to recognize the growth within relationships, to acknowledge when they nourish us and adapt when they do not. Relationships are dynamic entities, thriving on continuous investment and emotional availability.

Indeed, the role of empathy cannot be understated in the nurturing process. It allows us to step beyond our own perspectives, to truly see and feel the experiences of those we care about. Empathy acts as the bridge between individual experiences, fostering a sense of understanding and unity. When we listen with our hearts open, we cultivate a space where meaningful connections can deepen and flourish.

The act of nurturing bonds also demands a balance between investing in others and maintaining a sense of self. Often, we risk losing ourselves in the maze of others' expectations and needs. Embracing our own individuality while being part of a collective is a crucial component of maintaining healthy relationships. Self-care, personal boundaries, and assertive communication are instrumental in ensuring that relationships are not only supportive but also mutually enriching.

In nurturing bonds, we contribute not just to personal joy, but to the broader compassion that weaves through society. Strong interpersonal connections foster communities that are resilient and empathetic. They encourage cultures where understanding is valued over division and where differences are celebrated rather than criticized.

Every interaction holds the promise of a deepened relationship if approached with intention and care. Even casual acquaintanceships can transform into significant sources of support and empowerment when given the chance. So, as we embrace the complexity of our interconnected lives, we must remain mindful of the power we have in nurturing these bonds. Be it through thoughtful conversations, shared laughter, or simple acts of kindness, relationships are cultivated through moments that steep in sincerity.

As women take their place as architects of their destinies, nurturing bonds continue to serve as the touchstone of strength and support. Whether it's the wise counsel from a friend during times of trial or the encouraging words of a loved one that lifts us when we stumble, these connections are reminders that, despite the roles and responsibilities we juggle, we are never truly alone.

Let us continue to nurture these bonds, understanding that through them, we create not just a fabric of interwoven lives, but a legacy of love, resilience, and collective progress.

The Role of Empathy

Empathy is a bridge—a powerful connector that spans the gaps between individuals, transcending differences and creating a tapestry of mutual understanding. It's the essence of human connection, an ingredient often underappreciated yet remarkably transformative, especially in the diverse and complex realm of womanhood. In a world that sometimes feels divided and hurried, empathy invites us to pause and truly see each other, fostering relationships that are not only nurturing but also deeply authentic.

Imagine empathy as the gentle art of walking in someone else's shoes, feeling the unspoken sorrows and joys that accompany their journey. It's not about solving problems or giving advice; rather, it's about acknowledging another's reality and offering a compassionate presence. For women, who often navigate a myriad of roles and expectations, empathy can be both a refuge and a source of empowerment, allowing them to support one another in profound ways.

In relationships—whether familial, friendly, or romantic—empathy functions as a kind of emotional glue. It binds individuals together with threads of love, trust, and understanding. When a mother empathizes with her child's struggles, she fosters an environment where the child feels seen and valued. When partners embrace each other's vulnerabilities without judgment, they build a foundation of intimacy and respect that withstands the test of time.

Acknowledging another person's emotions and perspectives requires courage. It's an act that involves setting aside one's ego, silencing the urge to compare, and stepping into a place of vulnerability. Yet this vulnerability is not a weakness; it's a strength, a conduit for genuine connection. By opening oneself to the experiences of others, one can weave a rich and diverse tapestry of stories that enriches understanding and deepens personal growth.

For women, the act of empathy is especially significant. It nurtures a solidarity that is essential in tackling societal expectations and stereotypes. Empathy allows women to connect on levels that transcend superficial barriers, forming supportive networks that empower rather than compete. These connections are vital for personal and collective growth, providing avenues for shared wisdom and encouragement.

Throughout the world, stories of women coming together in empathy are abundant. In communities grappling with adversity, women have historically been the torchbearers of resilience, offering emotional support in times of crisis. Whether it's a circle of mothers in a rural village sharing resources and wisdom or a group of colleagues in a corporate setting fostering inclusive practices, the role of empathy is undeniable.

Empathy also challenges us to confront and dismantle our prejudices. It encourages a reexamination of narratives we hold about others, urging us to question stereotypes and assumptions. Through empathy, one can appreciate the rich diversity of experiences that womanhood encompasses, acknowledging that no single story is definitive. Each woman has her unique journey, shaped by her cultural, social, and personal circumstances.

This process of empathetic engagement extends beyond personal relationships. It spills over into our interactions with society and the world. Empathy informs our activism and advocacy, breathing life into efforts to create more equitable and inclusive environments. When women empathize with the struggles of others, it sparks movements that drive systemic change, inspiring a collective push toward a fairer, more compassionate society.

Yet, it's crucial to recognize that empathy is a skill—one that can be cultivated and honed. It starts with listening, really listening. This means being present, setting aside distractions, and tuning into not just words but the emotions and intentions behind them. It's about asking questions not to respond but to understand. It's about acknowledging that sometimes the most profound insights come from silence and presence rather than speeches.

In nurturing empathy, one learns to embrace differences, seeing them not as obstacles but as opportunities for deeper connection. It's about cherishing the mosaic of cultures, experiences, and perspectives each person brings into the relationship. This open-hearted approach enriches life in countless ways, filling it with varied voices that offer wisdom and joy.

In conclusion, empathy is not just a tool for connection; it is a force for transformation. For women navigating the complexities of modern life, empathy offers a pathway to more meaningful relationships and a more profound understanding of themselves and each other. It allows relationships to blossom—not by changing others but by embracing their essence. It's a testament to the strength found in vulnerability and the power of compassion to heal, empower, and illuminate the multifaceted nature of being a woman today.

Chapter 7:
Career and Ambition

In the labyrinth of career journeys, many women find themselves not just pursuing professions but forging paths that shatter the glass ceilings overhead. Ambitions are no longer confined to societal whispers dictating who one should be, but rather, they are self-defined, bold, and unapologetic. Each stride forward is a testament to resilience, born not out of mere desire but necessity—necessity to redefine success in a landscape that has long marginalized female ambition. These women stand firm in boardrooms, laboratories, classrooms, and fields, infusing spaces with creativity and passion that break convention. They're rewriting the rules, driving change with every job taken and every leadership position earned. It is in the aspirations and triumphs of these women that we witness the pulsating potential and transformative power of ambition, which fuels not just personal success but societal progress, elevating the narrative of what it means to lead with purpose and integrity today.

Shattering Ceilings

Throughout history, women have faced barriers, both seen and unseen, in the pursuit of their ambitions. Yet, these barriers have never defined their capabilities or dreams. As we delve into the domain of career and ambition, it's crucial to acknowledge that the journey of shattering ceilings is not simply about breaking through but about redefining what's possible from the ground up. For countless women, this path has been marked by determination, courage, and an unwavering belief in their own worth.

In today's world, the notion of a "glass ceiling" remains a powerful metaphor. It's a symbol of the invisible barriers that hinder women's advancement in their careers. But for many, it is also an invitation—a call to rise, challenge, and ultimately dismantle the status quo. The journey to shatter ceilings is layered and complex, often requiring women to navigate systemic biases while simultaneously cultivating their own strengths and resources.

The workplace, for many, has been both a battleground and a stage, where ambition and ability can shine. Women have entered fields once believed to be the sole terrain of men, redefining expectations with each step forward. The stories of women who have shattered ceilings serve as powerful compasses for those on similar paths today. They are stories of resilience, ingenuity, and triumph against the odds.

Consider the pioneers, those who've ventured where few women had gone before. These trailblazers didn't just open doors for themselves but held them wide for others to follow. Their journeys illustrate that breaking through isn't just about personal ambition; it's about creating bridges for the next generations. Professional landscapes have changed, in part, because of these audacious spirits who dared to see beyond limitations and envision new horizons.

But shattering ceilings isn't solely the pursuit of high-ranking positions or prestigious titles. For many women, it's about finding fulfillment and purpose in whatever work they choose. It's about owning their ambition without fear of judgment or reprisal, and it's about rewriting the narrative that ambition in women is contrary to femininity. In fact, it's deeply entwined with it.

Ambition, when nurtured, is a powerful force. When women embrace it, they not only transform their own lives but ignite a wave of change that challenges institutional structures. Sometimes, this means advocating for fair policies and practices in workplaces. Other times, it involves starting entrepreneurial ventures that disrupt markets and create spaces where women are celebrated, not just tolerated.

There is an undeniable power in mentoring and collaboration. Networks of support and sponsorship can become lifelines as women strive to reach new heights. By lifting each other up, women construct not just pathways but entire ecosystems where talent can thrive unfettered by bias. The stories of mentorship, both given and received, emphasize the collective strength found in shared visions and goals.

Personal stories, like those of women who have navigated the intricate dance of ambition and doubt, illuminate the heart of the struggle. These narratives are rich with insights, illustrating how resilience is born in the face of challenges. They remind us that ambition can be daunting and exhilarating, requiring not just courage but also adaptability and self-reflection.

As women continue to dismantle ceilings, they reshape industries, culture, and social norms. This transformative power is a testament to the capacity of women who refuse to be confined by tradition or expectation. It speaks to their endless creativity and the profound impact they have on the world. The journey is ongoing, with much work still to be done, but every ceiling shattered is a catalyst for change.

The path ahead involves both risk and reward, and there are moments of uncertainty alongside periods of undeniable progress. Society's perception of women's roles and capabilities continues to evolve, driven in part by the relentless momentum of those who have gone before and those who bravely step forward now. With each stride, the landscape of possibility broadens for women everywhere.

Ultimately, shattering ceilings is not only an individual pursuit but a collective endeavor. It's the cumulative act of challenging norms and creating new paradigms. To every woman who dares to dream beyond the limits set by others, remember: your ambition is not a burden—it's a beacon, lighting the way for those yet to begin their journey. Together, let's continue to shatter, rebuild, and transform, crafting a future where ceilings are a relic of the past and possibilities are boundless.

Redefining Success

In the dynamic landscape of career and ambition, success has often been depicted as a singular destination marked by wealth, status, and influence. Yet, for many women today, this traditional portrait fails to capture the richness and diversity of their experiences. The essence of redefining success lies in breaking free from these conventional molds and crafting a narrative that truly resonates with one's own values and aspirations.

For generations, the measuring stick of success in professional domains adhered to rigid parameters, often excluding the nuanced realities faced by women balancing multiple roles. The narrative that insists on a climb up the corporate ladder as the sole indicator of achievement dismisses the profound, albeit less visible, victories women achieve daily. These range from the courage to return to education later in life to the resilience shown when pivoting careers in pursuit of passion over paycheck.

For many women, the journey to redefine success starts with introspection. It's about asking deeply personal questions: What brings me joy? What kind of impact do I wish to have on the world? By grappling with these questions, women begin to sketch a vision of success that aligns with their personal values rather than society's prescribed benchmarks. Letting go of societal expectations can be liberating, yet it requires immense bravery to chart a path that is uniquely one's own.

Moreover, redefining success demands an understanding that achievements aren't always etched in grand gestures but are often found in everyday resilience. It's about acknowledging the quiet, ceaseless toil of single mothers juggling jobs, the mentorship provided by a woman thriving in a predominantly male industry, and even the collective strength of groups carving out space for female voices across diverse platforms. Each of these examples spins a new thread into the fabric of what it means to be successful.

Highlighted in personal stories are the tales of women who dared to deviate from the conventional script. Take, for instance, the entrepreneur who left a high-paying job to pursue a startup aimed at sustainability, choosing long-term impact over immediate financial reward. Or the teacher who dedicates herself to nurturing underserved communities, finding fulfillment in contribution over recognition. These narratives reflect a reframing of success as deeply personal and inherently diverse.

In this reshaping of ambition, community and connection emerge as central themes. One woman's triumph inspires another's journey, creating a ripple effect that challenges the status quo. Women are redefining success not just individually, but collectively, as they support one another in their ventures, celebrate each other's victories, and share in the inevitable setbacks. The shared understanding that success isn't a zero-sum game empowers a culture of mutual upliftment.

The push to redefine success also intersects with the broader fight for equity and inclusion in the workplace. As more women ascend to leadership positions, they're not merely occupying space—they're transforming it. By advocating for policies that support work-life balance, championing diversity, and mentoring the next generation of female leaders, these trailblazers are actively molding environments where diverse definitions of success are not only welcomed but encouraged.

Admittedly, this transformative journey is not without its challenges. Resistance from established systems and outdated mentalities can leave women feeling isolated or defeated. Yet, resilience is found in the shared stories of those who have navigated similar paths, who have broken barriers or created new models for success where none previously existed. In sharing these experiences, women both honor the progress made and acknowledge the road ahead.

As women continue to redefine success, they broaden the horizons for future generations. Young girls grow up witnessing a plethora of women forging diverse paths, understanding that their aspirations need not be constrained by predefined limits. The visibility of women succeeding on their own terms offers an expanded vision of post-pandemic possibilities, instilling a belief that success is as varied as the individuals themselves.

Ultimately, redefining success is about ownership—taking ownership of one's goals, achievements, and identity. It's a reclamation of narrative where each woman gets to decide what success means at different stages of her life. Whether it is leading a multinational corporation or nurturing a garden of dreams at home, each path is valid and valuable.

The narrative of success is changing, resonating with the voices of women from all walks of life and facets of society. It's an exciting, ongoing evolution, one that continues to inspire, empower, and embolden. Women are not just redefining what it means to be successful—they're revolutionizing it. And in doing so, they allow all of us to imagine a world where success is limitless, defined by personal joy and collective impact.

Chapter 8:
Body and Self-Image

In the dance of self-discovery, our bodies often emerge as both partners and battlegrounds. Women navigate a labyrinth of societal expectations about appearance, while also contending with personal perceptions that are shaped and reshaped by media, culture, and individual histories. It's in this intricate interplay of external pressures and internal dialogues where strength is forged. Embracing the beauty of one's unique form, rejecting the narrow molds that the world often prescribes, becomes an act of liberation and defiance. The journey to love oneself, wholly and unapologetically, is a testament to resilience. It's about standing in front of the mirror and seeing not just a reflection, but the story it tells—a narrative rich with diversity, courage, and undeniable power. Celebrating every scar, curve, and wrinkle as chapters of an epic tale, women are continually redefining what beauty looks like, and in doing so, reclaiming their narratives.

Celebrating Diversity

Embracing the rich tapestry of diversity in women's body and self-image is a celebration of uniqueness that uplifts and empowers. We live in a world adorned with kaleidoscopic differences, each woman carrying her own story, etched in the lines of her body, the hues of her skin, and the texture of her hair. This diversity is not merely a collection of varied appearances but a profound embodiment of experiences, cultures, and histories. Recognizing the beauty in these differences is an act of defiance against a world that often tries to confine womanhood to a single narrative.

In a society so frequently dominated by homogenized ideals, celebrating diversity requires courage and curiosity. It's about allowing the mosaic of womanhood to speak for itself, without interference or a need for translation. Every curve, every scar, every shade speaks of a journey - a testament to survival, adaptation, and individuality. This celebration isn't about comparing one to another but honoring each woman's path, which is uniquely hers yet part of a collective tapestry.

Diversity in self-image means acknowledging the power of difference not as an obstacle but as a strength. It involves understanding that our differences should be highlighted and appreciated, not scrutinized or diminished. Women come in all forms, with varied backgrounds and aspirations, making the spectrum of identity and beauty gloriously wide and all-encompassing. It's about dismantling the narrow confines of traditional beauty standards and opening our hearts and minds to the wonderful array of possibilities.

The narratives around body and self-image are further enhanced when we include voices from differing cultures and backgrounds. For too long, many of these voices have been disregarded or silenced, creating a monolithic view that doesn't reflect the true breadth of women's experiences. By amplifying these voices, we not only enrich our understanding but also pave the way for generations to embrace their authentic selves, free from the pressures of conforming to a singular notion of beauty.

Consider the transformative impact of seeing someone who looks like you, speaks like you, or shares your cultural markers being celebrated for their beauty and strength. It's a revolution of representation, breaking away from a history where mostly one type of beauty was idolized, often leaving others in the shadows. Visibility breeds acceptance, and acceptance fosters self-love. When we see ourselves represented positively, it cultivates an internal acceptance of our own selves, fostering confidence and engagement with the world.

And yet, celebrating diversity is not just about visibility. It's about education and empathy. It's about teaching each other and ourselves that while we may look different on the outside, our struggles with self-image are often universal. It's about sharing stories, listening with intent, and realizing that our beauty lies not in perfection but in the very elements that make us imperfectly human. The laughter lines that tell stories of joy and the stretch marks that speak of growth are all parts of this celebration.

This celebration finds power in vulnerability and authenticity. By revealing our truths and showing our real selves, we connect more deeply with others. As women embrace the diversity in their appearance and identity, they shatter illusions and dismantle fears tied to conforming to narrow standards. They pave the way for future generations to feel free in their own skins, highlighting that there is no singular way to be beautiful or to be a woman.

Celebrating diversity also demands broader systemic changes. It requires us to create environments that nurture and encourage diverse representations of women in media, arts, politics, and everyday life. Change must happen at every level—from personal perceptions to institutional policies. It calls for an active dismantling of barriers and an unwavering commitment to inclusivity, where every woman knows she is valued and seen for who she truly is.

Let's not forget the power of allyship in this celebration. Allies play a critical role by supporting diverse representations and standing against discrimination and marginalization. In every voice that joins the chorus of diversity, the melody grows stronger, echoing across divides and connecting us all in shared humanity. Allies help lift the voices that are too often silenced, ensuring that every woman feels her self-image, her identity, is respected and celebrated.

In conclusion, celebrating diversity in body and self-image is not just a personal journey but a communal one. It strengthens ties between communities, fosters understanding, and builds resilience. By valuing and promoting diversity, we craft a richer, more inclusive narrative of womanhood—one that recognizes the complex, wondrous layers of being a woman in today's world. This celebration is a call to bridge divides, honor distinct paths, and embrace the many forms of beauty and identity that define us. In doing so, we empower every woman to stand tall in her truth, resplendent in her individuality.

Challenging Beauty Standards

In a world saturated with images dictating how a woman should look, challenging beauty standards becomes an act of rebellion and self-empowerment. The quest for beauty is an intricate dance that oscillates between personal expression and societal dictate. It is both intimate and public, personal yet political. The pressure to conform can sometimes feel like an invisible hand, silently directing choices—from the clothes we wear to the colors we choose for our lips. However, the journey to redefine and resist these standards is one that is not only possible but essential for the liberation of women's self-image.

Historically, beauty standards have mirrored the societal norms and economic conditions of their time. In particular periods, certain body types or features were elevated as the ideal, only to evolve—or dissolve—as new eras unfolded. The curvaceous figures of the Renaissance, the boyish silhouettes of the 1920s, and the heroin chic of the '90s all tell stories of their own. Yet, amid all these evolving standards, lies a common denominator that quietly whispers: fit in or fade out. It's this undercurrent that women are now bravely confronting.

Reclaiming beauty away from mainstream molds requires courage. It's about seeing beauty in diversity—in every body type, skin tone, and texture. For many, it starts with unlearning: unraveling the belief systems that have long told us what is deemed beautiful. As we peel back the layers, there resides a more nuanced understanding of self, one that embraces imperfections as the unique markers of an individual journey. This shift away from a monolithic ideal opens up infinite possibilities for self-expression and acceptance.

Social media, both a friend and foe in this narrative, plays a pivotal role. On one hand, it can perpetuate unrealistic standards through heavily edited images and filtered realities. On the other, it provides a platform for voices that celebrate authenticity and advocate for inclusivity. Campaigns that promote body positivity and self-love resonate with many who are tired of the one-size-fits-all mentality. Influencers and everyday women alike are increasingly shedding these confines and showcasing beauty in myriad forms.

The drive to challenge these standards also stems from a desire to protect future generations. Parents, caregivers, and mentors have long grappled with how to foster healthy self-images in young minds in a world that constantly tells them they're not enough. By confronting and discussing these issues, we offer a narrative that's centered around self-worth, rather than mere appearance.

Moreover, challenging beauty standards isn't just a personal mission—it's a collective call to action. When a woman steps outside of these constraints and models authenticity, she doesn't just affirm her own identity; she paves the way for others. She disrupts the rigid frameworks that deny the diversity of womanhood, and by doing so, she encourages a more inclusive celebration of beauty.

Nevertheless, this journey is neither linear nor easy. It requires grappling with internalized notions of beauty, interrogating why certain ideals persist, and actively choosing to love oneself despite them. It's a journey that many women take, sometimes unknowingly, as they navigate the complexities of self-image throughout their lives.

In many ways, this challenge is as much about representation as it is about resistance. The more diverse representations become normalized, the less likely women are trapped by narrow confines. Movies, advertising, and fashion are beginning to reflect this slow but steady shift. There's an undeniable power in seeing oneself represented in the broader cultural narratives; it can be a salve to years of feeling unseen.

Even as globally conscious brands and media gradually make strides towards inclusivity, it's imperative that the story of beauty continues to be rewritten by individuals themselves. Armed with the knowledge of past struggles and present possibilities, each woman's redefinition of beauty acts as a ripple, contributing to a larger wave that factors diversity into mainstream understanding.

Ultimately, the ability to challenge and redefine beauty standards hinges on self-perception. It asks each woman to be the architect of her unique narrative—not just to see her beauty reflected in the mirror but to define it based on her terms. In doing so, beauty becomes not a destination, but a part of the ongoing journey of understanding oneself, forever evolving and ever-expanding.

This resilient challenge remains vital as it dovetails into broader conversations about body and self-image. It's about reclaiming agency over one's own narrative and celebrating the wonderfully diverse manifestations of womanhood. The fight to redefine beauty is merely one facet of a much larger quest toward self-acceptance and empowerment. Let's continue to build a world where women are celebrated for all that they are, unencumbered by arbitrary standards and free to embrace their authentic identities. With each step forward, we're not only reshaping our self-images but revolutionizing what it means to be beautiful.

Chapter 9:
Health and Well-being

Health and well-being weave an intricate tapestry, blending the threads of body, mind, and spirit. In a world that rarely pauses, prioritizing self-care becomes a radical act of defiance and empowerment. Navigating wellness is not a solitary journey but a communal endeavor where shared stories of resilience uplift and inspire. Ignoring societal pressures to fit prescriptive molds, women are carving out spaces for restorative health practices that honor their unique rhythms. Whether through yoga, meditation, or simply the joy of silence, women find strength in nurturing their inner worlds. Each small act of self-kindness reverberates through their lives, creating ripples of change that reveal the boundless potential of choosing oneself. Embrace this journey, for it is as diverse and vibrant as the women it serves, endlessly evolving and always personal.

Prioritizing Self-Care

More than just a buzzword, self-care is a vital, thriving concept that breathes life into our daily existence. In a world that often hurls demands at women from every direction, prioritizing self-care becomes an act of courage. It's about claiming the right to nurture oneself amidst expectations that often place women's needs at the periphery of their own lives. It's rejecting the myth that self-care is an indulgence, and embracing it as a core part of our identity and well-being.

Understanding self-care begins with a story—a story unique to each woman. In the chaos of life, self-care isn't a one-size-fits-all formula. It reflects our individuality, tied to our personal histories and desires. Perhaps it's as simple as sipping a cup of tea, enveloped in silence, or indulging in the guilty pleasure of a trashy novel. For some, it might be a challenging hike that pushes physical limits or finding solitude in painting that reveals unspoken emotions.

The journey of self-care is deeply personal, yet beautifully interconnected with the world's tapestry. Women around the globe practice self-care in unique ways, shaped by culture, environment, and circumstances. From Japanese forest bathing to the Italian art of "dolce far niente"—the sweetness of doing nothing—these practices teach us that self-care knows no borders. It integrates the wisdom of our ancestors with the aspirations of future generations, creating a bridge between the old and the new.

However, acknowledging the importance of self-care also means confronting the barriers preventing us from prioritizing it. In balancing careers, families, and commitments, women often succumb to the invisible labor expected from them. Self-care becomes a footnote, lurking on the to-do list, perpetually waiting for the 'right time.' But the right time never magically arrives. It takes intentional action to carve out space in our lives that honors rest, relaxation, and renewal.

Prioritizing self-care begins with challenging ingrained narratives. For too long, the whisper of guilt has followed women who dare prioritize themselves. It's time to shatter the myth that self-care is selfish. Instead, it should be recognized as the wellspring from which empowerment flows. When women invest in their wellness, they contribute more profoundly to their families, communities, and the world at large. It's a radical way to give back by first filling one's own cup.

Imagine a world where women listened to their inner selves without judgment. What if self-care wasn't just a weekend affair? Picture the power that emerges when women unapologetically claim the space they deserve. Resilient women, baring no shame in saying no to what depletes them, emerge stronger, ready to tackle challenges with renewed strength and clarity. Picture mothers teaching daughters that they're worthy of rest and care, breaking cycles that have long devalued women's needs.

The path to prioritizing self-care can be as varied as the women who walk it, but certain practices resonate universally. Mindfulness offers a gentle reminder that life isn't about rushing from one task to the next. It's in the moments between, where we find meaning and connection, where self-care takes root. Mindfulness anchors us, helping us become more attuned to our bodies and emotions, creating a pocket of calm in a whirlwind of activity.

Moreover, setting boundaries is a profound, necessary form of self-care. It's saying a firm yes to oneself and a necessary no to what drains us. Women who master the art of boundaries find freedom in their newfound space. They guard their time with fierce protectiveness, understanding that each boundary drawn is a step closer to sustaining their own health and joy. Boundaries teach others how to treat us as we learn to honor ourselves.

Societal change often begins in the personal realm. As women embrace the power of self-care, they become catalysts for broader cultural shifts. Community support is essential on this path. Women supporting women, encouraging rest and renewal, disrupt a cycle of burnout inherited over generations. Conversations about self-care should be as common as discussions about careers and relationships, normalizing the notion that to nurture oneself is to nurture the world.

Indeed, the landscape of self-care is ever-evolving, mirroring the dynamism of womanhood itself. As we navigate life's complexities, let's remember that self-care isn't just an act but a philosophy. It's the gentle unfolding of our own potential, a path that's unapologetically ours. By placing self-care at the heart of our lives, we not only honor ourselves but contribute to a legacy of empowered women standing strong, shoulders squared, ready to face the world unflinchingly.

Navigating Wellness

In the kaleidoscope of modern womanhood, the journey towards wellness is a path that many tread, albeit with diverse challenges and hopes. Seeking wellness is more than a trend; it's an essential quest for balance in a world that demands women to juggle innumerable roles with grace. It's about creating a harmony between the physical, mental, and emotional spheres, each feeding into the other, crafting a more profound sense of well-being.

Wellness isn't merely a destination you arrive at; it's an ongoing journey marked by introspection and self-awareness. Each woman's wellness path can look remarkably different, influenced by cultural backgrounds, personal experiences, and societal constructs. It's about understanding that wellness is inherently personal—a tapestry woven with threads of individual choice, barriers, and the empowerment that comes from making those choices.

The first step in navigating wellness lies in understanding one's own body and mind. Recognizing the signals your body sends—those whispers of fatigue, the tightening of stress, the elation from a good night's sleep. This awareness forms the bedrock of any wellness journey. It's crucial to listen to these signals, to understand and not merely hear. Feeling out of touch with these signals doesn't mean failure; instead, it highlights the areas where we might need a bit more love and attention.

Then, there's the mental aspect. Mental well-being is as integral as physical health. In a society that often rewards endurance over ease and busyness over balance, taking time for mental well-being can appear countercultural. Yet, it's vital. Practices like meditation, journaling, or therapy aren't one-size-fits-all; what revitalizes one woman may leave another unfulfilled. The key is exploration—allowing oneself the freedom to try, fail, and find what truly nourishes the soul.

Emotional wellness is arguably the most intricate part of this trifecta. It involves navigating the complex maze of feelings, both those that empower and those that challenge us. Emotionally resilient women know the power of vulnerability. Yet, allowing ourselves to be vulnerable in a world that can sometimes seem harsh requires immense courage. Building a support network of family, friends, and fellow women can provide the cushion needed to take those brave leaps into self-exploration.

Community plays a pivotal role in wellness. For many women, their journey towards well-being is buoyed by the support of others. Whether it's a book club, a yoga class, or an online community of like-minded individuals, sharing the journey fosters not only emotional support but also accountability and inspiration. It's a reminder that while wellness is deeply personal, it is never isolated.

An often-overlooked facet of wellness is its intersection with creativity. Engaging in creative endeavors—be it painting, writing, or even culinary arts—can serve as a cathartic outlet, a channel through which emotions and stresses can flow and dissipate. Creative expression invites joy and rejuvenation, often leading to surprising insights about oneself and the world.

Moreover, wellness is deeply rooted in the notion of self-care, a term that's evolved significantly over time. Today, it's understood as a comprehensive practice that ranges from the simplicity of a quiet bath to the structured routine of daily exercise. True self-care is about honoring what you need, when you need it. It's about rebuilding, not exhausting. It's the gentle art of setting boundaries that honor your needs, rather than stretching yourself to meet everyone else's.

Practically, wellness can often mean engaging with healthcare providers, not just when sick but as part of routine care. Building a relationship with practitioners who respect and listen to you is essential. This process can be daunting due to systemic issues in healthcare itself, which may not always cater accurately to women's needs. Advocate for yourself, approach appointments equipped with questions, and never shy away from seeking second opinions where necessary.

Nutrition, too, plays a pivotal role in the broader scope of wellness. It's not just about what you eat, but how you nourish your body and mind. Developing a relationship with food that honors health, aligns with bodily needs, and is free from guilt or shame is a revolutionary act for many women. It's crucial to dismantle narratives around diet that dictate measures of worthiness and instead embrace a model of nourishment based on inclusivity and enjoyment.

Of course, exercise can't be overlooked. However, it's essential to redefine what exercise means on an individual level. For some, this might mean hitting the gym regularly, while for others, it might be a peaceful walk in the park, a dance class, or even stretching on a living room floor. Exercise should help in achieving energy, strength, and joy—not exhaustion or punishment.

The journey of wellness isn't devoid of setbacks. There will be days when exhaustion wins, when self-doubt creeps in, or when stress feels insurmountable. Recognizing that these moments are part of the journey forms resilience. Rather than a sign of weakness, seeking help during these times is a profound act of strength and self-awareness.

Ultimately, navigating wellness as women means crafting a narrative that is entirely our own. It's about rejecting societal pressures that confine wellness to mere appearance or superficial measures, and instead embracing all facets of well-being with bravery and grace. As we venture down this path, one truth becomes evident: by prioritizing wellness, we not only heal ourselves but also pave the way for future generations. The journey might be uniquely personal, but its resonance carries the potential to inspire and empower beyond our individual scopes.

Chapter 10:
Leadership and Influence

As we transition into discussing leadership and influence, it's crucial to recognize that these aren't merely roles or titles but dynamic forces shaping our shared reality. Women leading today are redefining what influence looks like in profound ways, turning traditional notions on their heads and inviting others to do the same. With courage and empathy as their compass, they navigate through barriers and illuminate pathways for those who will follow. In spaces where women's voices were once whispers, they've grown into a chorus, vibrant and resolute. These leaders don't just occupy positions of power; they embody change, making choices that ripple into the community and beyond. It's in the everyday acts of influence, where one's authenticity and vision come alive, that true transformation begins. They remind us that leadership isn't about being fearless, but about daring to lead through fear, driving impact not just in boardrooms, but in hearts and minds, spurring a movement that's as inclusive as it is inspiring.

Women in Leadership

There's a quiet revolution unfolding, and at its heart are women who dare to lead. Women in leadership roles are no longer just breaking glass ceilings; they're rewriting entire narratives, creating new stories of courage and resilience. This is not merely about achieving positions of power, but about transforming spaces and mindsets. It's about leadership with empathy, wisdom, and a dash of intuition.

For centuries, society has wrestled with diverse notions of leadership. Often, leadership has been a space occupied predominantly by men, shadowed by narrow constructs and traditional constraints. But the landscape is shifting—the voices of women are echoing in boardrooms, bridging gaps, and catalyzing change. They're not just participating; they're influencing, reshaping the definition of leadership by infusing it with compassion and inclusivity.

Consider the remarkable journeys of women who've walked this path before us. Indra Nooyi, Oprah Winfrey, Angela Merkel—these are names that resonate globally. They have navigated labyrinths of adversity, each step seasoned with both grace and grit. Their stories teach us that leadership isn't just about the final destination; it's about the path and how one treads it. It's about the balancing act between vulnerability and authority, intuition and strategy.

One of the most critical aspects of women in leadership is mentorship. Mentorship is like a bridge, connecting generations and empowering those who dare to dream big. Women supporting women, offering guidance and wisdom, sow seeds for future leaders. It's in this nurturing environment that ambition is cultivated. Mentors help erase the word "impossible" from the lexicon of aspiring leaders, replacing it with "I'm possible."

The business world, once a male bastion, is witnessing a change. Corporations are learning the value of diverse leadership. Inclusion has transitioned from being a buzzword to a business imperative. Women leaders bring perspectives that were once sidelined. They highlight the importance of collaboration, expressing leadership that thrives not in isolation, but through collective effort. Their approach often emphasizes consensus-building and community, reshaping hierarchical management systems.

Indeed, women leaders face unique challenges. The path is often fraught with balancing societal expectations and personal aspirations. However, these challenges can serve as fuel, burning even stronger when faced head-on. Coco Chanel once said, "The most courageous act is still to think for yourself. Aloud." And this is precisely what women in leadership are doing today—amplifying their voices, acting as catalysts for a new era.

In the realm of politics, women are rising as power brokers and peacemakers. Leaders like Jacinda Ardern have illustrated the effectiveness of leading with kindness and empathy. Their success is not measured solely by their political achievements but by the trust and hope they instill in their people. These leaders are teaching the world that power and empathy can coexist harmoniously, and that true leadership is not about control but about service.

As we reflect on these evolving dynamics, it becomes evident that modern leadership demands authenticity. It calls for breaking away from the stereotypes that have long dictated what leadership should look like. Women leaders today must navigate a world laden with complexities, but with those complexities comes the opportunity for change. They redefine the playing field, transmuting obstacles into stepping stones.

While the journey towards gender equity in leadership is ongoing, the strides made cannot be ignored. They serve as a testament to what is possible when resilience meets opportunity. As more women rise to leadership positions, they bring with them a mosaic of ideas, experiences, and strategies that enrich organizations and societies alike.

The path to leadership for women is as diverse as the women themselves. Some may lead quietly, influencing through subtle acts of kindness and innovation. Others may stand at the podium, their voices rising above the noise to inspire and spark action. Each path is valid, each style valuable. The power of women in leadership lies in this diversity, in the strength found within differences.

Ultimately, women in leadership are not just changing offices or policies—they're inspiring a shift in how we envision leadership itself. They challenge the status quo, daring us to dream of a future where leadership is accessible, inclusive, and above all, powered by the collective potential of humanity.

The journey continues, propelled by the stories of those who've paved the way and those who will follow. Women in leadership will continue to be the architects of change, designing a future that not only demands fairness but celebrates it.

Making an Impact

Making an impact begins as an ember within, an internal revolution sparking bold actions and inspiring transformations. For women in leadership, impact is less about the titles they hold and more about the ripples they create in their communities, workplaces, and beyond. In a world fraught with challenges, the force of a woman's determination and empathy can guide profound change. This section delves into how women harness their unique qualities to leave an indelible mark on the world around them.

Leadership, in essence, isn't just about commanding a room. It's about fostering environments where diverse voices crescendo harmoniously. Women leaders bring with them an innate understanding of the importance of collaboration, seeing the individuals in their teams and nurturing potential until it flourishes. Through mentorship and advocacy, they create ecosystems where everyone has the chance to thrive. This nurturing quality becomes the cornerstone of their impactful presence.

Consider the stories of women who have rewritten the narratives of their industries or communities. They haven't just succeeded for themselves; they've paved pathways for others to follow. Women like these understand that real influence isn't a zero-sum game. It's about sharing victories and lifting others as they climb. Each triumph is a collective one, and each setback, an opportunity to learn and grow together. Their guidance, however subtle or overt, provides the scaffolding upon which future leaders build.

Empowerment and influence often sit at the confluence of empathy and resilience. Women embody this duality, displaying strength not just in enduring, but in transforming challenges into stepping stones for progress. Through lived experiences, they illuminate paths others haven't yet envisioned. This courage to chart the unseen, coupled with the ability to empathize deeply with others' struggles, creates a leadership style deeply rooted in understanding and inclusivity.

Real impact manifests in how these women navigate and dismantle the systemic barriers that persist in society. From breaking through glass ceilings to redefining what success looks like, their actions challenge long-standing norms and stereotypes. It's about rewriting the script, not just for themselves but for every woman who felt she didn't have a seat at the table. Each barrier they break is a light illuminating new hands in the dark, reaching out for the same opportunities to shine.

However, making an impact isn't only about grand gestures or headline-making achievements. It's woven into the everyday, often unseen interactions, where seeds of change are planted one conversation, one decision at a time. It is the quiet confidence of a woman leading by example, showing integrity and character in every facet of her life. These are the leaders who inspire loyalty and devotion simply by being true to the values they espouse.

In their spheres of influence, women use their voices not just for themselves but amplify the unheard ones. By standing up and speaking out, they hold spaces for dialogue that can lead to tangible improvements in policy and practice. It's here, at the intersection of passion and purpose, that real change occurs. Their voices become a rallying cry not just for awareness but for actionable solutions that uplift communities.

The impact of women in leadership also extends into the personal realms, encouraging others to embrace authenticity and pursue passions unapologetically. These women balance leadership with vulnerability, showcasing strength through transparency. In doing so, they craft a patchwork of humanity that brings people closer together. By sharing their journeys, complete with struggles and triumphs, they become beacons for others finding their way in complex landscapes.

Imagine the collective force of women empowered in leadership roles across all sectors and communities. Picture the cultural shift when every woman's potential is nurtured and her achievements celebrated. This is the potential of their impact—the promise of a more equitable and just world shaped by diverse perspectives and shared goals.

Ultimately, the essence of making an impact lies in recognizing and celebrating the unique contributions each individual can make. Women leaders cultivate cultures of inclusion, where everyone's strengths are valued and harnessed toward common objectives. Through this, they inspire a legacy of influence that extends well beyond their tenure, leaving trails for future generations to not only follow but expand upon.

In conclusion, making an impact is about embracing a leadership style that is as varied and expansive as womanhood itself. It is a call to action for women to continue disrupting, creating, and championing change in a world that so desperately needs it. As they navigate their leadership journeys, their stories of influence and impact will undoubtedly inspire countless others to rise and make a difference, too.

Chapter 11:
The Intersection of Womanhood

As we delve into the rich tapestry that defines womanhood, it's impossible to ignore how race, class, and gender weave together, creating a vibrant and sometimes challenging intersection. This juncture is where personal identity and societal structures meet, carrying stories of triumph, resilience, and the often-unheard voices of those marginalized by circumstance. Women from diverse backgrounds bring a unique perspective, each story a powerful testament to overcoming unequal systems while nurturing dreams and ambition. The intersection of these identities reminds us that womanhood isn't a singular experience but a mosaic of voices that lift and inspire. It's in these narratives where we find empathy's true power, recognizing that every woman's journey, though distinct, contributes to the greater collective strength. Let's embrace this complexity, celebrating how these convergences fortify and illuminate the path forward, empowering all women to stand strong in their truth, knowing their multifaceted identities are not burdens but badges of honor.

Race, Class, and Gender

In the beautiful mosaic of womanhood, race, class, and gender weave a tapestry that is both intricate and profound. Each thread represents a unique experience, layering one upon the other to create a vibrant narrative that refuses to be simplified. We can't isolate these threads; to do so would be to miss the fullness of this richly interconnected portrait. Instead, we find power and depth in acknowledging how deeply entwined they are in shaping the lives of women everywhere.

The intersection of race, class, and gender presents challenges but also offers avenues for strength and resilience. It's within these intersections that women often find the tools to break through barriers, redefining what is possible. As we explore these intersecting identities, we are reminded of the core truth: each woman's journey is distinct and noteworthy.

Consider the experience of a woman of color navigating professional environments traditionally dominated by a different racial demographic. Her race isn't just a backdrop; it's a lens through which each interaction is filtered. It's a whisper or a shout, sometimes both, reminding her of expectations placed upon her, yet she imbues the space with her authenticity, challenging the status quo simply by being herself.

Socioeconomic class intersects with these experiences by adding another layer of complexity. Economic structures can closely guard opportunities, often dictating who gets to the table and who remains outside the door. Yet, it's precisely this struggle that has fueled remarkable stories of persistence and ingenuity. Women across the socioeconomic spectrum innovate and uplift both themselves and their communities, crafting avenues for success where none seemed to exist.

The fascinating thing about gender, within these intersections, is its fluidity and culturally-imposed rigidity. The expectations of what it means to be a woman often shift depending on the interplay between race and class. In some spaces, femininity is celebrated; in others, it's subdued. Yet, in all cases, it's constantly being negotiated. This negotiation is not just about survival; it's also an act of rebellion and creation. By questioning and redefining gender norms, women chart paths that future generations will follow and widen.

It is vital, then, to listen to the myriad voices that rise from these intersections. When women speak about their lives, they give us invaluable insight into the multiplicity of the human experience. Through storytelling, the marginalized make their presence undeniable, crafting a narrative rich with lessons about resilience, hope, and transformation.

These stories become the bedrock for empathy and action. Recognizing the intersections of race, class, and gender within narratives allows for a broader understanding of the unique hurdles faced by many women. It provides a more comprehensive view of the world as it is and, importantly, as it could be. Embracing these stories challenges us to shift policies, change conversations, and create spaces where all women can thrive without the constraint of outdated norms.

Let's look at public figures who have navigated these intersections with grace and grit. Their journeys underscore the importance of representation. When young girls see themselves reflected in success stories of women like Kamala Harris or Malala Yousafzai, a crucial message of possibility is broadcasted. These figures don't just inspire; they validate experiences, opening minds to the prospect that the intersections between race, class, and gender are not hindrances, but strengths that can carry them through.

The journey of understanding these intersections is ongoing. It requires unrelenting empathy and the willingness to surrender preconceived notions. This exploration enriches our lives, engendering a deeper connection not only with others but with ourselves. It reminds us that the effort to understand, to hear, and to see is always worth it, for it propels us toward a world where every woman's experience is seen as essential and embraced for its uniqueness.

So, as we celebrate these intersections, we're reminded that the mosaic of womanhood is not just a picture; it is a living, breathing narrative that continues to evolve. Its strength lies in its diversity, and its future is as vast and limitless as the imagination.

Voices of the Marginalized

In the vibrant tapestry of womanhood, voices from the margins often carry a unique resonance. These voices, however quiet or unseen, hold stories of resilience, strength, and unyielding hope. It's in the uncharted territories of society that some of the most profound insights into womanhood emerge, offering perspectives that challenge prevailing narratives and unveil layers of identity often overlooked.

The conversation surrounding race, class, and gender can't be complete without acknowledging those who exist at their intersections. For the marginalized, their journeys are not merely about overcoming adversity but redefining the parameters of womanhood itself. They challenge the world not to see them as one-dimensional, but as individuals weaving complex identities. In this noise, the whisper of shared experiences becomes a powerful roar for change.

Women who navigate multiple identities often live on the brink of paradoxes. A Black woman may find herself wrestling with the cultural mandates of strength, all while seeking tender spaces to express vulnerability. Similarly, a Latina might juggle the warmth of familial expectations with the aspirations of personal ambitions. These complexities aren't burdens but rather the rich veins of experience that enrich the broader spectrum of womanhood.

Consider the narratives of indigenous women who stand as guardians of their communities and custodians of ancient traditions. Their stories tell of land, legacy, and a perennial struggle for rights. Through their stewardship of culture and their battle for recognition, they embody a form of leadership deeply rooted in resilience. In their resistance, there is a reclaiming of voice—a powerful antidote to historical erasure.

Migrant women also hold pivotal roles in this dialogue. They often face the stark challenges of new environments, language barriers, and economic instability. Yet, the immigrant journey is steeped in courage and the pursuit of better opportunities. Their stories are not just about transition but transformation. They remind us of the multiplicity of womanhood and its capacity to thrive amidst displacement and uncertainty.

Similarly, the voices of women with disabilities must be amplified. Society often defines them by their limitations rather than their possibilities. And yet, from these women, come stories of innovation, tenacity, and the quest for inclusion. Their experiences challenge the often narrow definitions of capability and redefine what it means to live fully.

In discussing marginalization, women of diverse sexual orientations and gender identities also step onto the stage. For them, the dance of womanhood twists through societal norms and expectations that don't always allow for their truth. By living authentically, they dismantle the walls of binary confines, expanding the understanding of gender and identity.

It is essential to listen and learn from these voices, not out of charity but out of respect for their unprecedented impact on society. Their stories are a call to action, urging others to listen actively and challenge the systemic structures that uphold inequality. By doing so, the pathway to a more inclusive understanding of womanhood is forged.

Bringing marginalized voices into the light enriches the broader discourse. Their narratives are not separate stories but essential threads in the narrative of womanhood. They offer a chance to see beyond societal constraints and to imagine a future where every woman, no matter her background, can be wholly seen and heard.

The intersectionality of womanhood is a reminder of both the diversity and the unity in the fight for equality. As these voices rise, they form a chorus, relentless in their pursuit of recognition and change. By sharing their unique perspectives, they empower not only themselves but generations to come—carving new definitions of strength, femininity, and what it truly means to belong.

Chapter 12:
The Future of Femininity

The future of femininity is an unfolding narrative rich with potential and transformation. As we stand at the nexus of change, today's women are redefining roles, tearing down outdated frameworks, and envisioning a world where femininity embraces freedom and fluidity like never before. There's a palpable shift as more voices join the conversation, encouraging authentic self-expression without the chains of societal constraints. Our collective vision for tomorrow is emboldened by the strength of diverse perspectives that knit together a tapestry of empowerment, understanding, and unity. Each story, each struggle, and triumph we share paves the way for future generations, imbuing them with the courage to shape their destinies. With open hearts and fierce determination, women everywhere are crafting a future where the complexity and beauty of femininity are celebrated in myriad forms, ensuring a legacy of resilience and hope.

Evolving Roles

In the dynamic landscape of today's world, the roles of women are constantly being rewritten, shaped by both external societal shifts and internal reflections. These evolving roles challenge the traditional molds that once limited women to a narrow sphere of expectations. Women today are stepping into spaces previously deemed inaccessible and are crafting paths that defy conventional wisdom. This transformation isn't solely about breaking barriers—it's about redefining the essence of roles that women can play, embracing a future where possibilities are boundless.

Consider the role of women in the workplace. Decades ago, certain professions were predominantly male-dominated, with women often relegated to roles considered more "appropriate" for their gender. Today, the script has flipped. Women are not only participating in these fields but are excelling and leading. This shift is more than a change in statistics; it's a profound paradigm transformation. It embodies the journey from being a part of the workforce to owning and shaping industries, proving time and again that competence and talent transcend gender.

In parallel, at home, traditional roles are undergoing a significant metamorphosis. The archetype of the female caretaker, while still revered, is now joined by a multitude of other roles women choose or need to fulfill. Today, it's about partnership and shared responsibilities, with both women and men redefining what family dynamics and domestic life look like. This change is not about devaluing the role of caregiving but rather about expanding the narrative to include a broader spectrum of experiences.

Social movements and activist voices have played a crucial role in spotlighting and accelerating these shifts. They push against the barriers of inequality and fight for justice and opportunity across multiple arenas. By amplifying the voices of women and placing the spotlight on systemic issues, these movements propel society towards greater inclusivity. As a result, women are increasingly finding platforms to express and showcase their multifaceted identities, driving change from within their communities and beyond.

Education has served as a pivotal catalyst in the evolution of women's roles. With increased access to education, women have not just chased dreams—they've shattered glass ceilings. From science to arts, to engineering and politics, women are not only participants but are leading thinkers and innovators. Education empowers women to dream big, believe in their potential, and act with conviction in pursuing their goals. This change is a testament to generations of struggle and advocacy for the right to education, highlighting that education is not only a key to personal success but a driving force for societal evolution.

While the women of today might stand on the shoulders of giants, they also bear the responsibility of paving new paths for future generations. These roles carry weight, with each decision potentially impacting those who come next. It's about fostering environments where young girls can see role models who look like them and know that they too can aspire beyond the boundaries set before. This responsibility means continuous growth, learning, and unlearning, challenging stereotypes and societal norms that hinder progress.

The digital age has introduced new dimensions to evolving roles, with technology acting as both a tool and a stage for change. From social media platforms where voices can be amplified globally at the click of a button, to tech innovation and entrepreneurship, women are carving niches and claiming spaces. Technology is democratizing opportunity, allowing women to network, build businesses, and nurture communities of support from their homes or anywhere in the world. This brings with it new challenges and opportunities; navigating digital landscapes demands a savvy that merges traditional knowledge with modern digital fluency.

As roles evolve, the importance of community and connection stands out more than ever. Women have supported each other across history, forming sisterhoods that provide strength and resilience. Now, this community is growing, encompassing networks that cross borders, time zones, and cultures. It's about shared experiences and collective progress, ensuring that as one woman climbs, she extends a hand to the next.

However, with evolving roles come challenges. Balancing these roles, whether it's in the personal, professional, or broader societal realms, is an ongoing dance. It's about finding harmony rather than perfection, understanding that evolving roles involve trial, error, triumph, and sometimes failure. It's the courage to begin again that keeps the journey alive.

The future of evolving roles is as much about adaptation as it is about intention. It demands a vision where opportunities are not limited by gender but are driven by passion, potential, and determination. Women everywhere are contributing to this narrative, contributing their voices, their experiences, and their successes to a future that is inclusive, diverse, and equitable.

The journey is not solely about individual change but about cultivating a world where different roles can coexist, harmonize, and intersect. As women continue to navigate the evolving tapestry of roles, they redefine femininity itself—shaping it not as a static ideal but as a dynamic, evolving force. In this evolution lies the promise of a future rich with possibilities, where every woman can write her own story, on her terms, and in her voice.

The past informs the present, and the present sets the stage for the future. Each stride forward is a testament to the strength, creativity, and resilience inherent in every woman, fueling the ongoing transformation of roles. As long as women continue to push boundaries and explore new horizons, the evolution of roles will remain a powerful narrative in the journey of femininity.

Vision for Tomorrow

Looking forward, the concept of femininity is not just expanding; it's transforming. In this shifting landscape, the possibilities are exhilarating and boundless. We find ourselves at the intersection of change, an era where women are not only reclaiming their narratives but also redefining what it means to be feminine. It's not just an evolution — it's a revolution.

In this future, the lines defining femininity will blur and broaden. No longer confined to traditional roles, women will have the freedom to shape their identities without societal limitations. They'll move beyond predefined scripts and create personal stories rich in diversity and uniqueness. Each woman will embody her version of femininity, whether that means pursuing a career, nurturing a family, or a combination of both and more.

Technology will play a pivotal role, bridging gaps across cultures and communities. It'll be a powerful tool for fostering global dialogues about womanhood. Imagine a world where a young girl in a remote village can connect with a mentor in a bustling city; where experiences and perspectives are shared instantly, fostering understanding and empathy on an unprecedented scale. The digital age will become an ally in amplifying female voices, ensuring they're no longer mere whispers but resonant echoes that ripple through society.

However, technology on its own isn't enough. The future of femininity will also hinge on education and awareness. As women gain knowledge and understanding of their own potentials, they'll be better equipped to challenge outdated norms and create new paradigms. Education will not only empower individuals but also communities, laying the groundwork for systemic change. Women will lead from the front, crafting policies and practices that reflect their realities and aspirations.

Even as femininity expands, the core of its evolution will be rooted in interconnectedness. Moving past competition to collaboration, women will recognize the strength in unity. By supporting one another, they'll build communities that thrive on shared successes and collective resilience. Mentorship, networking, and allyship will become cornerstones of this new era, ensuring that the ladders women climb are steady and built for others to ascend alongside them.

Leadership will take on a new face, one that emphasizes empathy and inclusivity. The future won't be about one-size-fits-all solutions but adaptable and diverse approaches that celebrate differences. Women in leadership roles will redefine success, shifting away from rigid hierarchies to more fluid and collaborative models. This leadership style will inspire not just women but all individuals to pursue authentic paths and contribute meaningfully to their environments.

The dialogues around femininity's future will also involve dismantling systems of inequality that have perpetuated gendered hierarchies. The vision for tomorrow requires addressing intersecting issues of race, class, and other social identifiers, advocating for comprehensive equality and justice. In building this future, these conversations will challenge deeply ingrained biases, creating spaces that are more inclusive and representative of all women's voices.

At the heart of this transformational journey will be the narratives women hold. By sharing their stories, triumphs, and struggles, they'll offer blueprints for survival, resilience, and joy. These stories will serve as reminders that femininity is not monolithic; it's a vast tapestry of lived experiences that deserve recognition and celebration. They'll fuel the momentum needed for lasting change, inspiring future generations to continue the legacy of courage and innovation.

In this emerging horizon, femininity will be a dynamic tapestry woven with threads of individuality and community. It will challenge us to think beyond binaries and embrace a spectrum of expressions and identities. The vision for tomorrow invites everyone — regardless of gender — to participate in constructing a world that cherishes diversity and nurtures femininity in all its complexity and splendor.

Ultimately, the future of femininity is bright and boundless. It's a call to action, a dream turned tangible through the collective efforts of women around the world. As boundaries shatter and horizons expand, women will step confidently into a future they've imagined and built for themselves, and for generations yet to come. And in doing so, they'll remind us all that to explore the vastness of femininity is to discover the infinite possibilities of human potential.

Conclusion

In weaving together the stories, perspectives, and insights contained within this book, we've embarked on a journey through the intricate tapestry of femininity. Each chapter offered a window into the myriad experiences that define womanhood, revealing both the shared threads and the unique patterns that make each story compelling. Now, as we draw these narratives to a close, let's reflect on the empowering essence that is being a woman in today's world.

Our exploration began with the quest to unravel identity, a journey marked by the courage to discover authenticity and the delicate art of balancing myriad roles. From personal narratives to cultural insights, the sheer richness of women's lives was brought vividly to life. It revealed a powerful truth: every woman writes her own story, resonating with diverse voices yet singing her own melody. This self-authored identity is not a static destination but an evolving journey—a vibrant testament to strength and resilience.

As we delved deeper, the power of stories emerged as a cornerstone of empowerment. Women sharing their narratives not only inspire others but also illuminate paths previously unexplored. These tales of triumph, struggle, wisdom, and growth remind us of the indomitable spirit that resides within every woman. By embracing and recounting these stories, women assert their place in a society that too often sidelines their voices.

Understanding womanhood from a cultural perspective brought into focus the ongoing dialogue between traditions and modernity.

While certain ideals persist across cultures, each narrative showcases the diverse ways women navigate and challenge these paradigms. Embracing change and fostering dialogue between the past and present is crucial for a future that is inclusive and empowering for all women.

In navigating society's expectations, the chapters highlighted the resilience required to break free from limiting norms and stereotypes. The stories showcased women who refuse to be confined by outdated conventions, choosing instead to redefine their roles. This ongoing battle for recognition and respect is not just personal; it contributes to a broader societal shift towards equality and understanding.

Personal growth and empowerment remain central themes, as they offer a transformative path towards inner strength and fulfillment. These tales of courage teach us that every change embraced and every obstacle overcome contributes to building a robust sense of self. The journey of personal growth is a testament to the resilience and tenacity that define women.

The heart of womanhood also lies in the relationships and connections built along the way. Through nurturing bonds and fostering empathy, women find strength in community and compassion. These relationships act as a support network that amplifies individual and collective voices, making it easier to navigate life's uncertainties.

Our discussions on career and ambition illustrated that women are not just participants in their professional lives; they are leaders, innovators, and changemakers. By challenging the status quo and redefining success, women empower future generations to dream bigger and break more barriers.

Body and self-image concerns were addressed with a celebration of diversity and a challenge to beauty standards. Emphasizing the importance of self-acceptance and authenticity, these narratives encourage women to love themselves as they are, fostering a sense of confidence and empowerment that is both liberating and transformative.

Health and well-being are foundational pillars upon which the strength of women is built. Prioritizing self-care and navigating wellness are not indulgences; they are essential acts of survival and resistance. This focus fosters a culture where wellness is accessible and integral to every woman's journey.

In leadership and influence, women are finding their voices, making an impact, and leading with authenticity. This is not limited to official roles but extends to all areas where women can inspire change and lead by example. Women's leadership is reshaping the world into a place that values compassion, collaboration, and resilience.

The intersection of womanhood with race, class, and gender provides a critical lens to understand the multifaceted nature of identity and experience. Voices of the marginalized demand space in the dialogue, advocating for a future that values all perspectives and drives towards true equality.

Looking ahead to the future of femininity, the evolving roles and vision for tomorrow paint an inspiring picture. Women continue to redefine what it means to be female in an ever-changing world, embracing roles that challenge old paradigms and ignite progress.

As we conclude, let this book serve as a reminder of the transformative power of storytelling, connection, and empowerment. May it inspire women everywhere to embrace their narratives, break barriers, and foster a world where every woman's voice is heard and cherished.

Further Resources and Readings

The journey of exploring and understanding femininity and womanhood is as vast and varied as the women who embark upon it. To dive deeper into these multifaceted identities, it's invaluable to seek out additional resources that challenge, inspire, and expand our perspectives.

Books

- *"We Should All Be Feminists" by Chimamanda Ngozi Adichie* - A compelling essay that redefines what it means to be a feminist in the 21st century.

- *"Untamed" by Glennon Doyle* - A memoir that encourages women to break free from societal expectations and embrace their true selves.

- *"The Beauty Myth" by Naomi Wolf* - An exploration of how beauty standards are used as a form of social control against women.

Articles and Journals

- "Mapping the Margins: Intersectionality, Identity Politics, and Violence Against Women of Color" by Kimberlé Crenshaw - *An essential read on intersectionality and its impact on the lives of women of color.*

- *"The Second Sex" by Simone de Beauvoir* - While controversial and complex, this foundational text remains relevant in discussions of existentialism and feminism.

- *"Why Women Still Can't Have It All" by Anne-Marie Slaughter* - A poignant piece challenging the idea of "having it all" in career and family life.

Podcasts

- *"The Guilty Feminist"* - A comedic yet insightful podcast that addresses the everyday challenges of being a feminist in a modern world.

- *"Call Your Girlfriend"* - A pod about the ins and outs of female friendships and careers, hosted by long-distance best friends.

Documentaries and Films

- *"Miss Representation"* - An examination of how media portrayals contribute to the underrepresentation of women in positions of power.

- *"RBG"* - A tribute to the life and legacy of Supreme Court Justice Ruth Bader Ginsburg and her influence on gender equality.

Organizations and Movements

- *The Global Fund for Women* - An organization advocating for gender equality and women's human rights around the world.

- *Lean In* - Founded by Sheryl Sandberg, this movement seeks to empower women to achieve their ambitions through community support and education.

Embracing the complexities of womanhood requires not just reflection but action and education. These readings and resources invite you to continue your exploration beyond the pages of this book, broadening the conversation and advocating for a future where every woman's voice can be heard and appreciated.